The Best
That
I Can Be

Timothy John Mason

The Derwent Press
Derbyshire
www.derwentpress.com

THE BEST I CAN BE
By
Timothy John Mason

© 2006 Timothy John Mason

All Rights Reserved.

ISBN 1-84667-024-1

Cover art and book design by:
Pam Marin-Kingsley
www.far-angel.com

Published in 2006 by

The Derwent Press
Derbyshire, England

www.derwentpress.com

Dedicated to the one true person I love in this world,

Claudia

For her undying love and dedication to me, without which
I am sure I wouldn't be where I am today.

Have you ever wondered what it's like living in a body that doesn't work properly? Maybe you're in the care industry, maybe you're a doctor or a nurse, maybe you are just curious, or maybe you just don't care. Either way, I hope you read on and get some insight into my new life.

PROLOGUE

I don't remember much in the early days, so forgive me if I generalise and have little information.

I enjoyed windsurfing and even had a go at kart racing, owning my own kart at one point. So, as you can see, I was quite active. I never dreamt what was going to happen would happen, but it did. I mean, how could you?

I was due to go to Rome, to live with my Italian girlfriend, Claudia (correctly pronounced Clowdia).

We then had a two year-old son, Giona (pronounced Jonah) between us, a very happy, intelligent little boy. He was Italian. He spent most of his talking time in Rome, Italy, although he did spend the first two years of his life over here. But now he lived constantly with his mum in Rome. Claudia didn't like it over here, she found the majority of English people very cold. I must admit there is a vast difference between English and Italian people. The Italians are so warm and friendly. I loved it there, she had a very close family and close circle of friends. Then, when we met, Claudia was 27. I was 40, but I looked and acted a lot younger, so I was often told. I had longish highlighted hair, I kept myself very fit, going to the gym most nights, running, rowing, skipping and weights, I was quite lean. Even when I went to Rome, I quite often went running. I did push-ups when I could and I was quite proud at my level of fitness.

I had been a hairdresser and business owner for the past six years. I hadn't done hairdressing all my life, I kind of fell into it in my late twenties, I seemed to have a natural flair for it. On paper, it was not a very good business, even though I was busy, but it paid cash and that gave me lots of time away. I had five working with me, a mixture of employed and self-employed. They were very good, looking after my business whilst I was gone, one even looking after my dog, who came with me into work every day and was everybody's friend, when they were offered a hot drink and an individually wrapped coffee biscuit.

I lived above the business, but as I said, I was going to sell the residence and move to Rome, to be with Claudia and Giona. I had already taken a car load of things over there, about two more to go. My plan was to keep the business in England. It provided us with a little income, which meant I would have to work part-time in Rome, to make up the shortfall. I had a dream, to bring back old small cars, which you could sell for a profit here, you had to bring about two or three over here, but I had all that worked out. I needed to sell about twelve a year.

I met Claudia whilst in a bar on holiday in The Sierra Nevada, Spain in August 2000. She is unusually beautiful. She is very slim and very well educated, including spoken and written English. I soon learnt that Claudia was very black and white. She called a spade a spade. For example, she was very involved in the "Don't attack Iraq" campaign. Claudia posses the same beauty as Barbara Streisand, she isn't obvious, but in her own way she is beautiful and she had a certain way about her. You have to see her to appreciate this. I was later to find out what a rock she is and how much I loved her. Some may say it all happened to quickly between us, but it felt right. Little did we know that life would be so cruel to us, before we really got to know each other. Children, of all ages, would flock to her and she would give them all her time. She was a wonderful mother, being loving, compassionate, very interested, strict and fair. Her parents were rocks too. Retired. The most wonderful grandparents (unlike mine).

I had an elder sister Jenny. She was six years older than me, married with three children. She lived in a village close to me.

I also had an elder brother, Jerry. Five years older. Married, with three children also. He was a Squadron Leader in the R.A.F. and was stationed in Cyprus. Later he retired and moved to Canada with his Canadian wife.

My father lived In East Sussex, but I had not spoken to him in years. We had fallen out over a trivial family matter, which was unresolved. I had tried to patch things up, but to no avail. I was sure he was influenced by his new wife.

My mother, who lived in Teignmouth, Devon, had a longstanding boyfriend. She had not remarried. She split up from my father in about 1983. She had an avid interest in flowers and dogs. Small dogs preferably.

I was kept hidden from Claudia's parents to start with. Well, I was a lot older, already with a son, and I was a hairdresser...

Claudia just had one brother, Stefano, who was married in September of 2002 to Aura (pronounced Owra).

Although Claudia was in Rome, Italy, I continued to court her and frequent trips to Rome soon ensued. I suppose I went over more than thirty times. I was a very lucky man.

I quite often went to Rome and I felt I had escaped the clutches of my ten year relationship with Julie. We had produced a son, Jacob, born April 1996.

He loves football and sweets, both traits, I am sure, which had nothing to do with me.

Although he was young, I constantly told Jacob I would be living in Rome, with his younger brother and, of course, Claudia. He accepted I would go, but I knew it would be difficult for me.

He was a lovely son and an incredible brother. He kept in touch with Giona. Every time I phoned, I gave the phone to him whenever he was with me and he went to Rome more than a dozen times, being totally accepted by Claudia's parents. His love for Claudia was so obvious and Claudia loved him dearly and when Giona came along, he loved him too.

I had had headaches and bouts of dizziness about two or three weeks before it happened and had complained to my doctor of a pain in my neck, which I constantly took pain killers for. The doctor had referred me for an eye test, the results of which they, the hospital, assured me were okay, although there was an anomaly with my peripheral vision, which they didn't investigate further. They said everything was normal.

I began writing this at Rowans Rehabilitation Unit, Plymouth. It is closed now, just part of the National Health Service cutbacks. I think they sold it and the land it stood on to property developers. No doubt it is worth more to them, as a potential housing estate, than what they originally acquired it for. Rowans has moved now to a much smaller unit and it is not called Rowans any more.

I began writing on my mobile phone, then, when I got my laptop, I wrote it on there, with just one finger, on my left hand. My right hand didn't function. Writing with my left was slow and my emotions got in the way on occasion, along with my spasms. Why did I start writing? I don't know is the answer to that. I hadn't written anything before. Maybe it was my way of coming to terms with what had happened, it certainly helped, or maybe I wrote in fear of my memory going. Perhaps it was my way to escape, to feel normal. I had so much to say, maybe writing substituted my speech. I had taught myself, over the years, to say things correctly, so writing was not difficult for me. I think my writing is simple and I have written this from the heart, so it is easy to read and understand.

I have tried to avoid names, but if you read it and you are my subject, you will know it is you, or you will know who I am talking about. So, a big thank you to all those that didn't know they were contributing to this book.

Just one thing, if you want to support me and you have borrowed this book, from family or friends, go out and get your own copy, you tight-fisted bastard!

I have been truthful as it's things that happened. Poignant, sad or funny, it's what I felt in my new life, so I hope you read on and enjoy it as much as I did when writing it.

CHAPTER ONE

I t was seven o'clock in the morning, Sunday 7th March, 2004. The mobile was ringing. I had left it on the floor the night before. I didn't have a house phone, as I could always use the one down-stairs in the salon. It must be Claudia phoning. Who else would call me at this time? I won't get it, I thought, as I lay next to my then seven year-old son, Jacob. He stayed with me every other weekend. I would phone later, when I was properly up. Little did I know that things could be different now, if only I had got that bloody phone. I contin-ued to doze. After all, it was Sunday and Jacob hadn't woken up yet.

It all happened around eight o'clock.

What the bloody hell was that? I thought. I began shaking. I could faintly hear Jacob shouting at me to stop, along with a distortion noise, like you get on a radio or television, which seemed to come from inside my head. I was shaking, uncontrollably.

I knew I was wetting myself. I looked down and saw the stain spread across my jeans. I must have got up and got dressed sometime. But I don't recall when it was. My seven year-old, who by this time was up, was naturally upset, except about the wetting myself bit, which he found quite amusing. It must have been the responsibility of having Jacob stay that kept me slightly compos mentis.

I managed to press the numbers on my mobile for Claudia. Jacob spoke. He told her in his own, seven year-old way that I was being silly. I began to come round and I was able to speak over the mobile to Claudia.

I spoke slowly and deliberately. At first, she thought I was putting on a voice, then she began to listen to me. I told her that I heard a noise in my head and how I couldn't move when this was happening. I don't know why, but I told her to remember that I felt normal before. I don't know why I told her this, I just did. It was as if I knew something was very wrong with me and I was going to pass out.

I told Claudia I was going to call the Emergency Services. Claudia didn't want me to be alone, so she suggested I call my sister Jenny or a friend of mine, Steve. Looking back, I suppose she thought I was just ill. She was soon to find out.

Next I called Jacob's mum, who lived about twenty minutes drive or about nine miles away. I said I didn't feel well and could Jacob go home. Although she said I didn't sound well, she didn't offer to come and get him.

No answer from my sister or Steve, I guess it was too early. Apparently, I called Claudia back, this time crying. I don't know where Jacob was at this time. I explained to her that my sister and Steve were not answering. Claudia was a little concerned. She hung up on me, as she wanted me to just call someone.

I was desperate. Who could I call to take Jacob? Who could I call that I could completely rely on?

I called Rachel, a work colleague of mine, to come and take Jacob home. I then called the Emergency Services. I must have known I was sick to do that. I told them I needed an ambulance. Within what seemed like minutes Rachel was there. She offered to take Jacob home, whilst her boyfriend Stuart stayed with me. Jacob picked up his things and went with her.

The ambulance crew arrived just after, which was quite lucky really, as I had what can only be described as a fit. I lay on the bed, uncontrollably shaking and a noise going on in my head, the same noise that I had before. I remember I could faintly hear one of the ambulance crew looking at me and trying to make a decision about my condition. That was all I remember. I don't recollect how I got off the bed, downstairs or the journey to the hospital. I must have blacked out.

I had had two strokes.

CHAPTER TWO

The technical term is an ischaemic, or infarct. It was discovered through an angiogram that I had a bleeding inside the lower part of the brain, the brain stem, which is responsible, mainly, for balance and co-ordinating muscle movement. This can be brought on by hypertension, heart disease, high cholesterol, diabetes, obesity, family history. To name but a few. None of which I had. I was fit and healthy, or so I thought. I was a little stressed from running my own business, but I thought that was normal. The stroke I had was not the normal stroke. Whether that was good or bad, I don't know. Time will tell. The artery in question was both restricted and dilated, along with a rupture of a blood vessel, which in turn had blocked an artery. The stroke was a big one.

The damage was done. It was a severe stroke.

Will I walk again? Will I regain some, or all, of what I had before? I would like to think so.

Just for the record, a stroke refers to brain tissue that has been starved of blood/oxygen and is left permanently damaged.

At first, I went to Torbay hospital, where I am informed, by my mother, that I stayed for just one day and night, before being moved to a more specialist unit at, Derriford hospital, situated on the outskirts of Plymouth, Devon, where, so I am told, I went into the Critical Unit first and was monitored continuously. I was on a ventilator to assist my breathing and I was there for about five or six days before being moved to the Intensive Care Unit. I didn't have far to go, as it was the same ward. Forgive the next bit, as I don't know if I was in Critical Care or Intensive Care.

Everybody was told by the doctors not to expect much recovery-wise. The eye movement that I had was probably it.

It was Jerry's idea to record things in the early days. That's how a diary was kept and written in by everyone that came to see me, but manly kept and written in by my mum. It was kept everyday for the first month, but it soon got forgotten. I did refer to it, though, for the first few pages of this book. My mother came regularly, every day at first, then every other day, then as my condition stabilised she came less.

A darkened room and a bleep in the ear. That's how they took your temperature. With a tympanic. I just remember it as gun-shaped object, which they, the nurses, shoved into your outer ear. Did they take me to another even darker room, where I was even closer to somebody? At, I presume, night time, I had the feeling that I was. For there were no windows and I was slightly out of it. I also had the feeling, again at sleep time, of being stacked, or taken to another level. We probably were not, again it was just a feeling I had.

One night I couldn't sleep and they took me, I'm sure, to yet another, darkened room, where I think, I heard a nurse say "....well, this is a turn up...." and "....we don't normally have this happen...."

I didn't know it, but I nearly died.

There are some days since when I wish I had died. Not just for the fact that I am disabled now, but for reasons that will become apparent later on.

It can get very, very depressing, stuck in a body that refuses to work properly. What has happened all seems like a bad dream and I quite often find myself asking the same question. Why me? I was so fit and healthy, or so I thought.

Everything seems too much trouble. If I had died, everyone around me would be better off, eventually, I am sure.

Claudia, Giona and Jacob could just get on with their lives. Yes, they would miss me, at first, but they would learn to cope without me and then I would just be a distant memory. That's what goes through your mind sometimes. But fate has decided that I live the rest of my life like this.

It was about this time that I started having very weird, very vivid dreams.

There were lorries, lots of them, they were almost blocking my way. They only came out when it was dark and they were all carrying market goods. I was lost in them and I was trying to sell my car and buy an English four wheel drive off-road vehicle.

In reality I had a small hatchback turbo diesel, which did the job, but I had decided I wanted a four wheel drive car as it was more robust for towing a trailer with the old small cars on it. I would get one if ever I got some money, which was a possibility as I was due to sell at least the property where I was living. I couldn't decide about the business, although fate had now played its part. I managed to find my way through the maze of lorries to a kind of car park.

Covering all of Europe with a kind of paper maché, because it made it safer. Safer because of the altitude. After all, Europe was higher in my dream and it was only safe for me at low altitudes. I had to even it out. Make it all level.

Escaping from onboard a kind of ship. I say kind of, because I imagined there was a floating hospital, from which I was trying to escape. I lay on a table, which was lowered for me, but I couldn't get off it. I made attempts to, but I just couldn't move.

I used to dream a lot of another world with Claudia.

There was a big type of office that I was trying to also escape from. A big building, with a research centre, where they tested me with various bits of equipment.

A hospital could be no further from the truth. I must have known what was going on.

5

An escape from the research centre, which ended up with some training shoes and then a game. The game, somehow, involved me being in a glass cage and there was a large wheel. I was given a choice of how long I wanted to be in this case. I think I chose three years. . Then I met Claudia on a small wooden boat. The boat was moored in a beautiful bay. I also persuaded Claudia to meet me at a city, which had been attacked by and subsequently invaded by Romans.

Funny, the tricks your mind plays on you.

It was where I lived, the city that is, and I had made a home on the fringes of a market, in my four wheel drive car. To stay alive, for in my dream I knew I was sick. I drank lots of water and kept cool. You could eat near the market, which we often did. Claudia and I often went places. We went to a beach with our grown up children, all three of them. Two sons, including Jacob, and a daughter. Funny, I thought I had two, both boys. Anyway, we went out when it was cooler. Cooler, because it was safer for me. Then we met Jacob, in a sort of tele-transport area. He was transported by me drinking lemonade and being in a certain place, at a certain time. Weird.

Another dream was me going on a hill, but where I imagined I lived it was quite often foggy. Not on the hill, but in the village where I lived.

Exploring, higher and higher, was another one. Going up in an uncharted land.

Yes, I had many such vivid dreams at this time. I guess I must have been unconscious.

CHAPTER THREE

I didn't know, what was going on. My face and head were very swollen, from the bleed. I couldn't see it, it is just what I was told by Jerry, who had flown in, in the early hours of the Monday. Claudia also arrived on the Monday.

Even when I was close to death, I was not visited by my father. Sad. In fact, he never ever visited me and two years plus on, he still hasn't come to see me. Like I said, it is sad. I prefer not to think of him, as if he doesn't exist.

Anyway, where was I? Oh yes, my story.

My first real recollection was of Claudia attempting to shave me, with a hospital razor. Not that sort, I wanted to scream. I looked all around me and realised I was in a hospital. I didn't know why, but I accepted it. I was calm. She should know that that is one of the bluntest razors to use, I thought to myself. She told me she was going to be the best girlfriend, which she undoubtedly is. Then I remember my brother reading from one of the trashy daily papers. My choice I have to say. My sister read me some poetry from, I think, two poets that sounded the same, but were born hundreds of years apart. So she told me. It was very vivid poetry and I pictured what was said to me in my mind. Listening to this, I had made a decision that I would write poetry or a story, if ever I got better. I imagined I was being read this in the garden of a public house that had a very special stream and you could buy glasses to drink this water, if you wished. Even then I could hear okay.

I cried when Claudia went back to Rome, for a few days, to see Giona. My brother took her to the station. Bus station, I think.

Taking turns, only two visitors at any one time. That was the rule. But it was Claudia mainly, with me every step of the way. Even if she was not there, I could feel her love.

7

My only method of communication was by blinking. Two or more for yes. One for no. I couldn't move.

Lots of bleeping in the I.C.U. That was all the monitoring equipment, I suppose. Monitoring you to make sure you didn't die or to let people know if you did. I slept a lot at this time. I suppose it was just the brain, trying to recover.

The constant clicking of the special ankle straps they put over your feet that went tight when they clicked. I suppose it was to keep the circulation going in your legs. To be honest, I don't know. I know I didn't like them, but I guess they served a purpose though.

Jerry leaning toward me, reassuring me, telling me everything was going to be okay.

I kept my eyes closed, a lot of the time. Whether that was on purpose, or by accident, or my condition, I don't know.

Jerry bought me a ghetto blaster, along with various CDs and some headphones. I didn't really use the headphones. The music was put on, very quietly, for me, especially at night. I had a television set up for me, by the nurses, not my own. I watched a video, about tigers, mainly.

I think someone died whilst I was on the I.C.U. I think I heard a doctor ask for a second opinion, then they, I presume, turned off whatever was keeping them alive. From that moment on I was scared of becoming one of their victims.

I wasn't really aware, but I had had a tracheostomy or trachy for short, at some point. A pipe coming out of your lower throat, the other end being attached to a breathing machine. It used to make a "glug, glug" sound at times. Condensation just building up if you lifted the pipe up, the "glug, glug" sound would go away to another part of the machinery, I guess. The noise kept me awake some nights, because I had no way of communicating the problem to a nurse and they just didn't notice.

I think I remember the room where I had the operation for the trachy though. It was dark, very dark and full of televisions. There was a snowboarding programme on, which the doctor kept controlling, much to my annoyance. I was particularly interested, because it came from Italy.

I liked anything Italian. It changed to a cycling programme. They drugged you, I think and hope. But, everything was in my imagination. My mind was playing tricks on me.

Every now and again, throughout my experience here and on the next ward, the senior nurses or the physiotherapists would check the fluid level on my chest. They did this by first disconnecting the trachy, then inserting a tube in the hole that the trachy left in my neck. The tube went down to my chest and collected any fluid, if there was any. It would make me cough and then they listened with a stethoscope, to see if there was more fluid. If there was, they repeated this procedure again. Did it hurt? I coughed, didn't I?

It's funny, how you accept things. I sort of knew something was wrong with me, but I went along with everything that was done. I didn't scream or struggle.

I also had a Percutaneous Endoscopic Gastronomy, or P.E.G., which fed me direct to the stomach. I was wheeled, on my bed, to the operation area. A cork type of object was placed in my mouth, just before the operation.

Claudia came and went, to and from Rome, for there was Giona to see. I was more stable now, so they moved me upstairs at Derriford, I.C.U. and all I had was the trachy. The nurses commented on my cough, saying it was very strong. That's about it from the area I was in, for everything else is a haze.

CHAPTER FOUR

T hey moved me from the main I.C.U. on the Wednesday, just one and a half weeks after my initial accident, because I was doing so well, to a ward.

It all seemed like months to me.

The ward they put me on, was Meldon. A Neuro High Dependency Unit or H.D.U.

I didn't like it there, although most of the nurses were sympathetic. I just guess I was more alert and awake by this time. I had my own room, with a view. A view of a wall that is. But at least I had a window. I imagined it, first room by another ward and by some doors. I was close. It was the first room alright, but right by the nurses' station. It seemed like Claudia was always there, by my bed that is.

I am sure that one day I was taken to a shop area. My eyes were tightly closed, so I could only hear sounds. I am sure I heard people ordering their lunch, maybe I was dreaming.

Jerry had bought me a television, tuned it and meticulously set it up. The television also had a built-in video. They gave me a smaller trachy, which delighted everyone, as I started making more noises. My skin healed and closed up around it okay. They talked of me speaking when I was to have the trachy completely removed.

I always looked forward to the physiotherapist coming to see me. He was a he and Welsh, not his fault (being Welsh), and from what I saw knew his stuff. He was quite often escorted and he took great delight in pushing and pulling my legs and arms. They ordered me some special splints, fluffy, as it turned out, to go on my ankle and foot, to prevent my ankles from dropping. I also had an inflatable splint on my right arm to prevent the muscle from shortening, as it came in, naturally, by tone. The arm splint was inflated with a kind of bicycle pump. One day the arm splint was put on wrong and over inflated. Boy, did it hurt! I screamed and screamed. Claudia had gone for a coffee, with a good friend of mine. She was livid when she came back and sought out the ward Sister, demanding to know who had put it on.

One night I couldn't sleep. I indicated with my eyes that I was scared. My friend volunteered to stay with me. A senior nurse came to reassure me.

I had the trachy removed, which was quite a milestone and at first they just put me on a little oxygen that was through a mask, but that was cut down and soon removed.

By the end of March, the physiotherapists got me sitting out in a chair. Not for long. Thirty minutes at first, then it was gradually built up. They achieved this by using a battery-powered hoist, with a sling attached, which they managed to place under you. When the sling was hoisted up, you sort of sat in the sling, in a reclined position. The first time they hoisted me, I cried. Even though Claudia was there to reassure and comfort me. It was very emotional for me.

I managed to splatter blue rice pudding all over the speech therapist that came to see me. Just why it was blue, I don't know. I laughed a lot. They later discovered I was emotionally labile (pronounced lay-bile). It means I had no control over my emotions. When I cried, boy did I cry and when I laughed, I laughed a lot. I laughed at anything. I even laughed when I didn't mean to laugh, which was very annoying, as it just set people off. They just didn't understand that it was a medical problem. They just thought I was being funny.

It was the beginning of April; I had my first visitors, colleagues from the salon. I don't remember seeing them. Hearing them, yes, but not seeing them. I was quite emotional.

I was asked if I wanted to see a friend, whom I hadn't seen for years. I blinked yes. The more, the merrier and so began my visiting.

11

About this time I was also shown how to communicate with an E-Trans frame. Quite simple really. A frame made out of clear Perspex. On the Perspex was laid out the alphabet, in six colours, in each corner, in groups of six. Y and Z being on their own in the middle at the bottom. Along with six coloured circles. Each circle being a different colour. It was identical on the back. The idea was the receiver would look through the hole in the middle, align my eyes and get me, first, to look at a group of letters and then look at a coloured circle and, hey presto, I was able to communicate. Incidentally, only my eyes moved, I still couldn't move my head, or could my neck support it.

Crude, I know, but I began to rely on this board. It went with me everywhere. Anyone that held it was called the receiver, Claudia was the best at being the receiver. Others tried, but Claudia was definitely the best.

I ate some chocolate Easter Sunday. I was not supposed to and I took great pleasure, the following week, in informing the speech therapist. It wasn't much, a grain really. But I had some chocolate, it was from Claudia and it tasted like heaven.

I was moving my head, a little yes and no. No was easier, but I was nodding my head.

I definitely didn't like it on Meldon and couldn't wait to leave. My prayers were answered, for on the 14th April I was moved to Rowans Rehabilitation Unit

The night before Claudia was busy packing my things. Cards, a teddy bear, a cuddly monkey given to me by my eldest niece, who had come from Bishops Stortford just to see me.

CHAPTER FIVE

The ambulance came to pick me up. It was a sunny day and sun poured through the window of the ambulance and warmed my face as I lay in the stretcher.

It was a short journey to Rowans, as it was in the same site as the hospital.

A nice room I was given, right next to the nurses' station, to which there was an adjoining window so they could see me and a view of grass and trees out of the main window that I could see out of. There were two. It was a single storey, flat building. I soon made, or rather Claudia who met me there soon made it a home from home, with my cards on the wall. About forty and the rest of my trinkets were put on the shelf, window ledge or just hanging up.

I was soon assigned a physiotherapist, an occupational therapist (OT for short) and a key worker, whom I was to see if I had a problem. The key worker was my physiotherapist. I already had a speech therapist.

I was very emotional the day Claudia went back to Rome. I was aware she was going back. Using the board, I made it known to my sister that I was pissed off. I didn't want her to go. She had to, of course.

I soon settled into life at Rowans. It was to be my home for the next seven months.

I still didn't really know what had happened to me. It hadn't sunk in.

I had physiotherapy each day, along with speech therapy.

My mother bought me a bird table, so I could see the birds from my bed. All I saw was bloody pigeons. I hate pigeons. They used to crap all over where I lived.

I screamed and cried at the pain in my legs, especially my right leg. The doctor gave me medication for this. When Claudia was with me, she constantly massaged my legs.

It still seemed like she was always there. I obviously still had no concept of time.

It was after I had been there about three or four months that I started to realise what had happened to me.

Apparently I quite often asked the nurses to read the diary, although I have no recollection of this.

You always knew it was me coming into a room as I hiccupped very loudly. They went, eventually, but it caused me great discomfort as they were very violent when I got them, which was quite often. The laughing was a big problem and always interfered with my daily activities.

Apart from being emotionally labile, I dribbled a lot, my legs were in spasm, I couldn't move at all and I couldn't speak. I was embarrassed.

I felt strong enough, emotionally, to see Jacob in early May. Claudia was already over, so she prepared him before he came. He duly came, I duly cried. I was very, very emotional. He drew me a picture. He was very understanding. Claudia was there, to use the board or whatever. I had made a decision to see Jacob, the first few times, in bed. I thought it was best, for me, anyway. After all, a bed is a bed, but a wheelchair means you are disabled. I couldn't face that.

I think it was on Jacobs's second visit that I moved my left wrist, only a bit, but I did move my wrist. Someone had to hold my arm up for me to do this. He cheered his approval. I was amazed at how accepting he was of my situation. I originally started moving my thumb, only a bit at first, then it got stronger.

The OTs set me up with a possum – a gadget that controlled the television, on, off, the channels and the volume and the nurse call system, by remote, by my head, which was moving a lot more now, turning to the left (I could not move my head to the right) and hitting a switch that was set up. It was awkward to set up, as the switch was on a telescopic stand that kept moving when I hit it.

The nurse call alarm, which was set up on the possum, was very loud and easily attracted someone's attention.

I'm not sure when Jerry went back to Cyprus. After the first weekend I got to Rowans, I think.

Late April I started mouthing some letters, much to everyone's surprise. I started to get stronger.

Progress seemed all too slow for me, as did each day. Days were long and weeks seemed like months, especially when Claudia went back to Rome. She did teach Jacob to use the E-Trans frame and he became very good at it.

I was alone when she was gone but, she had to go back to be with Giona, who had been staying with Claudia's parents. I didn't see him, as he was too young to understand my situation and what with my lability, he might get upset, so it was best for him to stay in Rome. I saw friends when Claudia wasn't there, but it wasn't the same. I guess it was very hard for her in those early days. I had visitors, but I just wanted Claudia 24/7.

The OTs got me another wheelchair and a headrest that turned right. It was L-shaped and made especially for me. My head was badly contorted over to the right and needed constant support.

Claudia pushed me outside in my wheelchair and I saw, for the first time, my reflection in a window. I hated how I looked. We counted the number of people on a bus. It was a test of how good my eye-sight was – crafty.

It was a small room, about ten feet by nine feet, big enough to place a single bed in, with an en-suite bathroom, which consisted of a toilet, a sink, a chest of drawers and a wardrobe. Each morning we (there seemed to be about seventeen of us at any one time, the maximum being twenty-one) were offered a shower, which I took, initially, on a shower trolley. A bed made of plastic, with sides they could put up or down. They got you onto the trolley by rolling you first one way then the other, placing a specially designed sheet under you, a slip sheet (I guess it got its name because it was slippery), then physically pulling you from the bed onto the trolley, which they later pulled from under you. When you were on the shower trolley and the sheet removed, two of them would take you to the shower room. It took three people to move me onto the shower trolley, one either side of me and one to control my legs, to make sure they were not left behind. The trolleys would just fit in the shower room. I guess if you were a giant, your head would stick out. Even me, I was too big for the shower trolley, I am five foot eleven, or I was. It hurt my ankles, I moaned at being uncomfortable. Once, because my ankles stuck out over the end of the trolley, my left foot was burned on the tap!

I eventually progressed onto a shower chair. It reclined, so it was quite comfortable. Then, depending how I went, it was a reverse coming back, then they would get me dressed. I was always asked what I wanted to wear and I would nod my approval at the trousers or t-shirt that was held up. Then, when I was dressed, I would be hoisted into my wheelchair.

At night, they gave me most of my food. A liquid form of nutrition, called Ensure-plus, it came in 500 millilitre sized bottles, of which I had three through my PEG via a drip that bleeped when it was time to change the bottles over. I was also given Ensure-plus as a bolus, that's an extra, large amount, about 200 millilitres, at various times through the day, by pouring it in a syringe, which they had attached to my PEG. A plunger was rarely used. It looked like tea, but it did come in different flavours, which I could taste only if I burped, when I was given a bolus. An extra large quantity that is.

Once I laughed so much, I don't know why, that my stomach muscles tightened and as the nurse was trying to put the bolus in, it all started coming out along with the contents of my stomach, yeuch. The more I laughed, because by then I found it funny, the more I tensed my tummy, the more that came out.

In speech therapy, I was shown a mirror, which was used occasionally. I hated that mirror. It was used mainly to show me my lips and the way I was forming letters. I started off having to do aaa, eee and ooo. The speech therapist was very careful that I just saw my lips, in case the sight of a disabled me was too much. I did see myself. I didn't like what I saw, but I did see myself.

I got a new possum, with a big red switch, which I could easily control with the left side of my head. I couldn't tilt my head to the left very easily – that's why the switch was positioned on my left, it was a form of exercise. As my neck muscles were short down the right, it was more comfortable for my head to be turned that way. I still couldn't move myself, so I was rolled from side to side to get dressed and hoisted into my chair. It was an electric hoist, similar to what the physiotherapists used at the hospital previously.

I couldn't sleep when Claudia went back to Rome, so they assigned me a young nurse for a week to monitor my sleep. I had little sleep or kept waking up throughout the night.

Despite the brain damage that had occurred, my mind seemed to work okay though, which was a good thing, as there were people around me who didn't have a mind.

The OTs were trying to get me an electric wheelchair to test, with a view to getting me one. It was nice of them to try and get me an electric wheelchair, but why me? Was it their opinion that I would always need a wheelchair? Was it their opinion I would always be severely disabled? If so, they hadn't told me.

In physiotherapy, I was getting daily stretches. Monday to Friday that is and they recommended that I have a football between my knees, as my legs were so tight and the knees pressed together. This helped significantly. Plus I was going on the tilt table, which was a bed that electronically tilted up to 90 degrees. Using the board, I managed to say "I was so fit and healthy, why me?", to which there is no answer of course.

My physiotherapist changed. She left, which meant my key worker had left too. It soon changed to my speech therapist, a mature lady, who took an active role in my wellbeing at the Rowans Unit.

I started to get movement in my left, mainly my left arm and hand.

Every other day, was my bowel day, which I hated. One older nurse, I am sure, loved sticking suppositories up your bottom, or was it mine? They always rolled you to the left, which I hated, I don't know why, but I couldn't bear rolling to my left. They had to roll you that way, as it is something to do with your bowels, I think. Then, nine times out of ten, they would roll you back and then they would leave you for twenty minutes, so you got a result, then come back and clean you up.

The nurses got you up and dressed between half-past ten and twelve, depending on who was working. One, in particular, seemed more efficient at it than the others. She made me laugh. Once when she made me laugh, I choked and coughed so much I was violently sick. I thought I was going to die. It was only later that a nurse revealed to me that that was one of the senior nurse's fears. They showered me down and I was okay.

The seat on the shower chair broke in half one morning, with me on it. I didn't fall right through, but I was uncomfortable. I saw the funny side and people joked about it into the next day.

Teeth were cleaned every morning and in between cleaning, suction was used if you couldn't spit. Suction was a hard interchangeable plastic tube, attached to a flexible one, which was attached to a machine that sucked.

I was given a wet shave every morning, more often than not whilst I was being showered and I managed to convey to visitors what type of razor they should get me. I went to bed about seven. I didn't wear anything, I slept naked (Commando, they call it) mainly because I get very hot in bed. One nurse seemed more organised than the rest and was able to get me up earlier. That was the one I liked. One of the patients was hard of hearing, and for a while he was in the next room and she used to shout at him, which made me laugh. Even when he eventually moved right down the end, you could still hear her shouting at him – all in good spirit.

I had physiotherapy every afternoon. I went down to them on a shower trolley at first and was hauled over to a plinth. Later I went in a chair, which they got me out of by first removing the sides and then sliding me over on to the plinth, by using a banana board. A banana board bridges the gap between two places and is curved, hence its name, and you are just simply slid over, still in the sitting position. It would take three of them to do this and was quite awkward, as I had no strength in my arm to help them.

Eventually I was transferred with a Standaid, which was easier for them and me. They pushed and pulled my muscles, to maintain the movement, which I have to say I enjoyed. I had no pain anywhere really, except in the inside of my right elbow joint when my arm was straightened.

The new physiotherapist that was assigned to me had some good ideas for me and worked hard at my rehabilitation. She measured all my muscle movement on a points system, one being little or no movement, five being normal. My muscles varied, but it was about two to three on my left upper limbs and about zero to two on the rest.

Also in physiotherapy they would sit me in my chair, with a table in front of me, straighten my arms out, predominately my left arm, and help me sweep it across the table. They placed objects under my arm, like a tissue or a towel, to reduce the friction. Such was my movement then. They placed balls of various sizes under my left hand, when I was in various positions, to encourage some movement, but my hand would just flop off. I had normal feeling in all my limbs, they just wouldn't work.

Because my ankles were a little floppy, I would go on tiptoe whenever I was hoisted up and my foot wasn't flat, the physiotherapists made me some ankle splints out of a sort of Plaster of Paris. My toes would just stick out and it would go to just under my knees. The physiotherapists would struggle to hold my ankle in the right position while it set. I had a few of these, the idea being to improve the angle of my ankle each time. The plan was I would keep them on for a few days at a time. They were very uncomfortable and I had some of them cut off in the early hours of the morning.

I don't know when it was, but I developed a fear of heights. Claudia was there. I started feeling very unsafe on the tilt table, like I was falling forward. I sort of began waving. Claudia thought I wanted a cuddle. I started making a noise and the physiotherapists and Claudia soon realised there was something wrong. The tilt table was lowered, but I had developed a fear of heights which was to stay with me for some time to come. I was even scared of height on television, anything that showed height I just could not watch.

As it was nice (it was summer), Claudia took me into the courtyard they had. We would phone Giona and Claudia would tilt the mobile phone to my ear so I could hear him talking. He talked in Italian, as he didn't know any English.

The OT decided to try me out on a shower chair, which had a cut-out hole and doubled as a commode. I also went to the toilet on this. A purpose-made cardboard bowl was fitted into it and I always asked if I could be hoisted on immediately, as I discovered that the suppositories did their job very quickly.

I screamed when I went to the hydrotherapy pool, being winched up on a chair, the height was just too much for me. The three physio-

20

therapists decided between them that it was best to abandon going in the pool, as I was so worked up. I always had three physiotherapists with me when I went. Even being rolled in the bed was scary. I went back to the pool, staff permitting, later. I found that my performance on the stationary bike was better on the days I went to the hydrotherapy pool. I don't really know why, but it was. I would float around a bit, courtesy of some strategically placed long buoyancy aids. Once, I even stood up and my feet were nudged forward, so I could take a few steps. Later on, after about two weeks, I tried standing by using a Standaid, which was successful.

A Standaid, of which there are many types, literally helps you to stand. The principle is the same for all of them. A strap goes round your upper back, which Is then attached to the hoist part of the Standaid. That part is then raised automatically and lifts you up. Your feet are left firmly on the machine. You can hold on. Not everybody can use it, the muscles in your legs need to work. You can get straps that go round you that support your hips as well, but the physiotherapists found out that I didn't need to use that.

My new physiotherapist was young as well. I don't recall the age of my first physiotherapist, but my second one was about twenty. They were good friends outside Rowans, running and going to the gym together, both of them being female.

My left foot splint was altered. I had got permanent plastic ones by this time. The heel and sole first, then the leg part was angled slightly as I was standing to one side and my left foot was turning over whenever I was in the Standaid for any length of time.

I had two lots of foot splints, day and night ones. The night ones were the fluffy ones I got on the Meldon ward. I was normally very good, keeping my night splints on all night, so long as they were not done up too tight. I kept my day splints on all day, unless they were hurting, then I had a break from them for an hour or two.

I also had an arm splint made for my right arm, as in the prone position my right hand would continually brush my neck and chin, which was very uncomfortable. I wore this at night, for an hour. I could only manage about an hour, as it stretched and hurt the inside of my elbow. It was made of a type of Plaster of Paris that automatically hardened on contact with air, cut and fastened with a crepe dressing, which was wrapped around it.

My scalp was itchy and hypersensitive. When washed or brushed, I jumped violently. It even just made me jump at any time.

It is hard for you that one day you can do anything, the next you can do nothing for yourself. You just have to accept it, it's just the way life has become.

Eventually, the nurses were told by the physiotherapists that they could use the Standaid to get me up in the morning and to put me to bed at night.

I don't know why, but when I got tired I pulled a funny face, which can best be described as a rabbit face. I mainly did this at night, when I was put to bed and in the mornings, when I was got up.

Claudia's brother and wife came over from Rome to see me. We didn't really go out, just stayed in the grounds of Rowans.

When my mum came to visit, she often bought lilies, which filled the room with their pungent fragrance. I later developed a great liking for them. My sister came when she could and gently massaged lavender oil in my face and body. I stunk. It was nice, but boy did I stink!

CHAPTER SIX

I gave power of attorney to Claudia and my friend, as I still had my hairdressing salon to take care of, even if it was up for sale.

Claudia had discovered that I had sent an erotic text, in my former life. To me it did not mean anything, I was just playing, but to Claudia I had broken her trust, I had wandered out of the relationship and that had made her very, very upset and angry. The text had stayed on the mobile phone, which she now had. I tried to lie my way out of it, but that just made matters worse and Claudia could see I was lying. Just why I had done it, I don't really know. I guess, just because I could. I was very happy, to say the least, with Claudia. Why then, did I risk my life with her? I suppose I was just lonely. I had been living in a caravan, for a while, until my flat, which I rented out, became vacant, as I had been letting it just before my strokes and I suppose loneliness played a big part, along with vulnerability. Oh, if I could turn the clock back... But I couldn't, could I? I just got carried away.

The last thing I wanted was for Claudia to go away from me. Thanks to me and what I did, she regularly went to a psychotherapist, when back in Rome. I was faithful to her, but that wasn't the point. As I said, I had broken her trust. Claudia quizzed me many times over the subject. I was very upset. Not for the fact that she had discovered my error, but for upsetting her. I had been very stupid and paid the price. I didn't like that she had discovered a bad side of me. I felt very guilty and hated myself, for a long time to come, I wanted to die. She asked me to open up and tell her everything, as that was what real partners did. The guilty feeling wasn't going to ever go away and it didn't. I was to suffer for it later.

I was regularly visited by friends, every other day, I suppose. When Claudia was over, she would come normally just before lunch and stay until eight or nine o'clock.

Derry, who was technically my dog, was bought to see me by Rachel, one of my friends, who he now lived with. Quite often I jumped when he woofed and although it was amusing to everybody else, it was hiding a problem that would manifest itself in the not too distant future. Derry was a tri-colour border collie of about eleven or twelve years. Some months before my strokes, because I was constantly going over to Rome and because of my future plans, I asked Rachel if she would give him a home. She readily agreed, because she had looked after him on many occasions.

As I could only use my front teeth and my swallow wasn't very strong, I was tested on food regularly and it was agreed by the speech therapists that I was ready for a puree diet. A puree diet is standard food, but highly liquidised. For dessert I had mostly ice cream. I was fed by a nurse or by my mother, who came twice a week, or by Claudia. How much I had upset her or how deep the hurt went, I don't know. I only know I had offended her deeply. At first, I could only eat lying down, so I went back to bed for all my meals.

I had expressed my wish to go to Rome. But just how practical that was, was left in the hands of my key worker, my social worker and, of course, Claudia. Italy didn't have a National Health Service or a Social Services, so I wouldn't receive any benefits, so life would be hard. Being here was hard, I didn't have Claudia or Giona around me. I couldn't watch him grow up.

I saw a psychotherapist, who I opened up to. I told him of my fears of losing Claudia. He assured me that she would always support me. I told him of my guilt, he assured me more and told me that feeling guilty was only natural.

My speech therapist changed to a young girl. I liked her attitude very much. I still kept my key worker though.

I had thickened drinks, through a spouted beaker. Two spoons of thickener to each 200 millilitre cup.

But I was topped up as necessary through my PEG.

Because I was eating and drinking so well, I had my PEG taken out. I waited a long time for the operation. I was originally told half ten, but I was kept waiting until half twelve, then I was wheeled in to see the anaesthetist, who asked me my name and a couple of other questions. I was able to nod yes, and then I don't remember any more.

I was not allowed any food twelve hours before the operation and twelve hours after. Before was no problem, but after meant I missed dinner and tea. So I had a bowl of Ready Oats at two in the morning.

I tried the electric wheelchair for one week and I felt lost when it was taken away. I was given an ordinary "push" wheelchair, which was a bit of a disappointment.

Claudia sent me a text from Italy to congratulate me about having the PEG taken out. It was calculated from my body weight that I needed to drink at least two litres of fluid per day. I guess the calculation was done by taking my height and weight into consideration. I found two litres difficult, as I wasn't used to drinking that much, so I devised a plan. A cup was 200 millilitres, so if I drank three cups each mealtime, that is 1800 millilitres in total, I could easily drink a cup or two through the day or night and so it was I had one cup before my meal and two cups after. I was only allowed cold drinks.

All my food and drink had to be recorded on a chart, so they knew what I had to eat and drink. I have to say that the nurses forgot on occasions, but I knew what I had had. I quite often reminded them to write it down.

I had two friends that mostly came to see me twice a week. They supplied me with DVDs for my TV. Pirate copies mostly. I never really asked how they got them, I just kept quiet about it and was grateful that I could watch the latest cinema releases, even if the odd head appeared, in the DVD, of the watching audience occasionally. One of them bought his laptop and a computer game that we all played. They were like a comedy duo with one constantly ridiculing the other. They were like a Laurel and Hardy team. They bought me, between them, a DVD player.

I complained that I was seeing double. More so to the left. I was booked in for an eye test. From those results, I went to a hospital actually in Plymouth, escorted and pushed by a nurse. I had various tests and I complained of not only the double vision, but everything up close was blurred too. I was given a prescription for reading glasses. They decided that for things further away, I didn't really need glasses and as for my double vision to the sides, it only really became a problem if I got double vision when I looked straight ahead, so they advised me to make sure I was always facing in the direction I was looking.

It was a nice day when the local optician came, who had been recommended and subsequently contacted. One of those rare, hot summer English days. We all sat outside, in the shade. I say all, because Claudia was over. I tried on various frames, until I decided on a blue frame. I also asked about and eventually had Reaction lenses that went darker in the sun.

Claudia quite often got me to try and straighten my legs. First one and then the other. I could lift the left leg a little way, but moving the right leg was hard, if I moved it at all. I liked just doing things for Claudia. I liked to make her happy. Then she would stretch both arms, the right being a lot more difficult than the left.

I had a T-roll or T-bar on loan from the physiotherapists, which I used at night, or any time I was on the bed. Basically it's a circular T shape that is padded and goes under your knees, with the down part of the "T", sticking up between your knees to keep your legs apart. The idea is that the bit that goes under your knees helps counteract the spasming and breaks the pattern in your legs. I couldn't bear not having the T-roll under my knees, it was very comfortable.

I longed for conventional food and quite often drooled when Claudia or Jacob ate in front of me. I got lucky one day. Jacob was eating some chocolate buttons and I looked longingly at them, then at Jacob, then back to the buttons. Jacob gave me about five and I was able to bite them, using my front teeth.

I not only drooled a lot, but because of my lability I sort of half laughed and half spat. I just couldn't control it.

I opened my bowels every other day, without any intervention now. I was taken straight to the toilet on the Standaid, which was lowered carefully so I was in the right position, and then the nurses left me. Still attached to the Standaid, so I was quite safe. When I had finished, I pulled the call bell which was on a cord and placed within easy reach of my left hand, and then the nurses would come back. They raised me back up and cleaned my bum. It's hard that you can't do it yourself, a very personal thing that you have to let others do for you and you have to accept it. It's humiliating, but it's just the way things are. The same as messing yourself, which I did on occasions and someone else cleaning you up. It's degrading, but you just have to learn to accept it. It's their job. I think the first word anyone understood was "Sorry".

Whenever Claudia was over, she regularly brought and spent time with Jacob. When the weather was nice, we went out the side of the building, so Jacob could play football. She looked so funny, kicking the ball, jumping each time she went to kick the ball.

I was very concerned about my weight. I wasn't big, but I noticed I was putting on weight and me being me, I decided just to have one pudding a day.

At last, I got my electric wheelchair, which was set on slow in all gears until I got used to it. The controls, which I could only just reach, had been placed on the left, as an extension of the armrest. It was mainly black and had a headrest and side supports, which snugly fitted as I had no movement in my trunk, they kept me up square and prevented me from leaning over. Because it tilted and reclined, I found that I could have my meals in the chair, if I reclined the chair back a bit. I choked on occasion, but eventually I used less and less recline. I needed a bit or the foot rests jammed the front wheels when I turned, or when I manoeuvred myself back. How did I know how much I needed? I counted in my mind. If I counted up to eight, whilst

I operated the tilt that was about right to clear the foot rests, the maximum being about twenty.

Monday mornings were funny, you had to be seen by the doctor, on their weekly rounds, by your bed, or in it. It felt like military school, or something out of a "Carry On" film. The doctor would ask you if you were ok and discuss you and any problems you might have with his entourage.

Blood pressure and pulse were taken weekly. My blood pressure was normal, but my pulse was about in the high seventies to low eighties. It was my goal that my pulse return to normal, which was high sixties to low seventies. It took just over a year for that to happen, but it did. I digress, now where was I? Oh, yes.

Weighing was neat, you were weighed once a week. Before, I was put on the bed and a stretcher like object was put underneath you, it had bars which could slide in and out the stretcher sheet. Once on the stretcher, and with the bars in place, you were attached to a weighing hoist and lifted just clear of the bed. Now though, they had scales you could actually drive onto in your wheelchair. The weight of your empty wheelchair was taken first, like at night when you were in bed and when you drove on to the scales, the weight of the wheelchair was taken off, which was kept on your wheelchair and they got your weight.

I only ate breakfast in bed. That was three drinks and a bowl of Ready Oats. I was only allowed Ready Oats because of my weak swallow.

One weekend morning, I ordered and got two warm, black coffees with two sugars. It was lovely but when I ordered it again, the following morning, I was told that it had to be approved and noted by the speech therapist, which it was not. I found that anything slightly hot, was too hot and I just couldn't eat it, or drink it. On the Monday I was tested on the coffee and it was duly noted.

I regularly had a urine test, to make sure my bladder was completely emptying between me weeing. A specialist nurse would use a mobile scanner, similar to those used in pregnancy, to scan my bladder and see how much urine I had. She used some gel to make the connection between skin and machine, which was always cold, but I didn't mind. Then I would have a wee in a bottle. Then she would scan my bladder again, to find out how much was in there, then it was a simple case of maths.

I had an offer for my business and the property. I was very happy, but it dragged on and dragged on and eventually fell through.

Because I had some movement in my left arm and I could grip with my left hand, albeit weakly, the OTs tried to get me to use a special spoon. It had a big handle and to make it easier for me, it curved toward my mouth. I found it so difficult to angle the spoon towards my mouth and the spoon kept tilting, so if there were any food on it, it would fall off. It seemed an impossible task.

I don't really know when it began, but one of the side effects of having my strokes, of which there were many, was I grinded my teeth a lot. It was when I was very tired, it happened mainly in the morning. I couldn't help it, it was automatic. The same as yawning, that was a side effect that I just couldn't control, I wasn't tired, but onlookers thought I was. I communicated to one and all that I wasn't tired, but more often than not they forgot. How annoying.

When I sneezed, boy did I sneeze! If I was on the Standaid, or on the loo, my legs would shoot back. If I was eating I would spray my food over impossible distances. I would make a such a mess.

My solicitor, who was also a good friend, came to see me and told me the good news. I had had critical illness cover on my mortgage and the lenders had paid out. I paid most of that into my building society. I did give ten thousand to Claudia, which she only used as travel expenses and I kept some in my personal account, which could easily be drawn on.

CHAPTER SEVEN

C alled "Conveens," they went over your manhood, and were rolled on. They were like thick condoms with a hole in the end, and had a special adhesive on the inside, which kept them on. They directed your urine via a tube into a leg bag that was strapped just below your knee that needed emptying through the day. The conveens regularly leaked, back flow they called it, or it came off altogether. I had these. Then I progressed onto bottles, they were cardboard. It was embarrassing really, as a nurse had to "place" the bottle. I had an itchy groin, which didn't help matters. I had one "placed" between my "tight" legs when I went to bed. Because they were made of cardboard, they didn't look much like bottles by the morning

Weeing was a very urgent affair. When I needed to go, I needed to go immediately. I had lots of times of being wet, both in bed, where I spent most of my time and out in my wheelchair. I had little control over my bladder and the night staff would "place" a bottle, just in case I got caught short at night.

Then the doctor told me I had a urine infection. I wasn't passing all my urine, It was pooling in my bladder, which is not a good thing as it leads to infection. So, I was given a catheter. I was lucky, because when it came to the time of changing my catheter, the nurses could not do it. Which meant I was back on conveens, which is a good thing.

By this time, I was using my left hand on the possum quite successfully, so long as it was positioned in the right place for my left hand to get it. I was drinking out of a spouted beaker. I didn't drink it myself because, I couldn't lift my arm that high. It was the kind of beaker, which a very young child would use so they don't make a mess. Still thickened though. It was tipped by a nurse so I could drink it.

The OTs quite often came in with the physiotherapists in the gym. One day I pointed out to both of them that parts of my right fingers and the right side of my face were a little numb. I still had total feeling, but they were a little numb. I think they told me that it was to be expected. The speech therapist tried me on a communication aid, which is a small portable key pad, about six inches by twelve inches, that says whatever you write into it and displays it on one line, scrolling along if necessary. You can store on it, so you can prepare sentences. When I first got it, I memorised all sorts of swear words. It would amuse me hearing it swear. It was not designed for that.

It sat on a folder and was placed on my lap each morning. They initially thought I would need one that scrolled through the alphabet that was on a stand and therefore couldn't be transported, but through the dexterity of my left hand I had an ordinary key pad. I just needed support for my left wrist, well I did on the Friday. By the Monday I did not need the wrist support, as I was able to use the communication aid unaided.

The arm splint was getting very tatty and, after me nagging a few times, the physiotherapists ordered a new one. It was a proper one, which was fastened with Velcro. I found it quite annoying, not that I didn't like to wear it, but because nurses and therapists alike would try to put it on backwards. It only went one way, on the inside of the arm. Not on the outside, like inexperienced people tried to put it on. I used the communication aid to convey that it went on the inside of the arm, but they still tried their hardest to put it on the outside. Many was the time I was left screaming, because they didn't understand how to put it on. I got frustrated and screamed with anyone, even Claudia, if I wasn't understood. I couldn't help it, it's just one of the side effects of having the stroke.

The OTs made me a hand splint, which I wore at night. It kept my hand in an open position and it was fixed by some special material, which acted as straps, onto some strategically placed Velcro.

I found I could support my head more. I relied on the headrest less and less until I stopped using it completely, then it was taken off. Due to a shortening of the neck muscles, I still couldn't tilt my head to the left.

At night, I used to go down to the front, where they had a purpose built reception desk, on top of which was another piece of wood. This acted as a sort of barrier to visitors and gave privacy to the receptionists and somewhere for them to place things, like their computer, I could just grab the lip of this, pulling myself forward, to strengthen my left arm.

One day it was very hot outside, so I said no to a top and went outside to sit in the sun, just in my shorts. When I had been out a while, I was approached by the doctor, who told me off about being in the sun and that I should at least have some suntan lotion on. I raced back to my room, to get my communication aid, hotly pursued by the doctor. I told him I already had sun tan lotion on.

Some friends bought me a mobile phone and I was able to keep in touch with people, by texting. It was also placed on the folder, next to the communication aid. This bought memories back for Claudia, but I am sure she could see the benefit of having it. Friends text me quite often, but I especially liked receiving a text from Claudia. It made me feel not so alone. Claudia was not good at sending texts, it is just how she was. Some days were harder than others for texting. I just could not press the buttons right, you know, three times for a letter "C" etc.

The only difference I really noticed in me, apart from what I have already mentioned, was the fact that I got very frustrated. This made me scream and cry. Not being able to speak and put my point across was, well, very frustrating.

As I got used to the communication aid, I used the board less and less, until the writer completely replaced it.

Because I was using the communication aid so well, I ordered a laptop computer, which I was able to use with mainly one finger on the left hand. I left the choice of laptop to my friend. He ordered one of the latest laptops you could get, it cost enough. The laptop was difficult for me to use, my left arm would tire and I would make lots of mistakes. The laptop was placed on a table and then put in front of me.

The speech therapist regularly monitored my swallow and food consistency, until I was able to eat mashed or finely cut food using my left hand and a conventional spoon, not the special spoon I had been practicing with, I refused that. I eventually went to a fork, as I personally didn't like the idea of a spoon. I was very shaky and choked a lot. I was always supervised. This opened up a whole new world for me in food, as I was able to eat anything. I always ate in my room, as sitting with others was just too much. I tried it once and coughed and spluttered my food everywhere.

Going to hydrotherapy meant going in the ambulance and guiding my wheel chair in was not easy.

I pleaded with the speech therapist that I could go down to one and a half thickeners and after testing my swallow, she agreed. They listened for clearance of a swallow, with a stethoscope. Drinks were still given me, as I still couldn't lift my arm up enough to tip the cup.

I was told that I was making a remarkable recovery and I was very lucky. I did not think so, on both accounts.

I broke down and cried in the corridor and a nurse had to take me back to my room. There was no reason for it, I guess everything had just got too much for me. She spoke to me about life and how she could never understand my situation and to be strong as I had come a long way.

As I said, there are some days when I just want to give up. It all becomes too much. Not having Claudia constantly by my side is difficult. She is my strength. My reason to go on. I cry a lot. I want my life back. I yearn to be with Claudia.

They had a garden and I regularly went out. A mainly paved area, with a funny raised garden. I say funny, because it was about four foot high and horseshoe shaped. I went to bed later and later, my regular time was eleven o'clock. Sometimes it was later than that, so I was not missed the day I was shut out in the garden.

I mainly sat on my own, choosing solitude rather than mixing with the other patients. I preferred it that way.

They had regular meetings, about every six weeks that is, all the people that were involved with me, including me, about my progress and my future at Rowans.

Claudia was in attendance for most of these and she spoke out very boldly.

I crashed quite frequently in my new chair. Once, I took out a cupboard door. On another occasion the wheels caught the bottom of my door when I was on my way out of my room, completely ripping the metal foot protector off. It didn't help that I laughed. Both were accidents of course!

In OT I was lifting and turning funny round discs up a kind of stand, rather like a mug tree, along with playing lots of large Chinese chequers, for my reach. I won most games, unless I was playing Claudia. Boy, she is good at that game, but if I challenged her to "Connect four" or "Four in a row" I would win every time.

I got up to about twenty minutes standing in the Standaid, but the staff could never get me back far enough in my chair, until they discovered that if they completely removed the strap, when I was standing, then lowered me. As it went down, I was able to straighten my arms, which not only gave them a good stretch but I could sit back further in my chair.

34

I was strong enough to hold on with both hands, so long as some-one put my right hand in the gripping position. My left arm and hand functioned nearly normally, but it got tired quickly and was very weak.

I also went on an exercise bike regularly, which I could use from the chair. I was able to exercise both arms and legs, although not at the same time. It went round on its own and I was either strapped in, or strapped on, depending on what I was doing. I had fifteen minute sessions. It had a small readout screen to show what you were doing and afterwards it would show what you had done. I could easily mon-itor my progress on the exercise bike. Some days were good and I improved. Some days were bad and I got upset with myself. I was very pleased with myself the day I did over four kilometres. I sent a text to Claudia about my great achievement.

Speech was my favourite though. In speech, I practiced everyday words. Some words were easier than others. I said things very quietly and my breathing was very shallow.

Although there was no real explanation, I found I could speak better when I was in the prone position and if I had anything to say, I fully tilted and fully reclined the chair. Speaking was important for me. Perhaps that's why I liked it. Although, at times I got frustrated, and then I couldn't speak the rest of the time. Normally I was able to communicate effectively with people using the communication aid and speech, where possible. I did not have access to the internet, but the speech therapist offered the use of her home computer for e-mails by copying mine to disc and taking the destination e-mail address.

I started on bisc-weet there. By the time I got to it, it was soggy and okay for me to eat. The speech therapist recommended that I could tip my own cup, which caused a few arguments. Not that I did-n't want to do it myself, but I was used to some one doing it for me.

I went with Claudia down to Derriford hospital. It was a busy place, which as a city hospital I suppose it would be. It had shops and a coffee area. I ate some chocolate buttons. We went to the Intensive

35

Care Unit and the High Dependency Unit where I had been. I was not emotional when I visited where I had been, but I did remember some of the nurses. The chair slowly made its way back up the hill. Boy, it was slow.

When Claudia was over here, we ate mainly in the OTs' kitchen. I was quite good, except for the time my then eight year-old was there (he had had a birthday). He found my laugh very amusing and I made such a mess with my food. My lability was worse when anybody laughed, which made it impossible for me to eat and drink.

Because of my lability I laughed a lot and some nurses took this as a cue to act silly around me, which made me laugh more and made them act even sillier. But I wasn't laughing at them, it was my lability.

I was taking a muscle relaxant through the day, and at night my legs were so tight. I was also given an antidepressant. I took an aspirin in the morning to thin the blood and so reduce the chance of having further strokes and I had an injection in my tummy every day, an anticoagulant. It helped prevent thrombosis. I hated the injection.

I had been on the anticoagulant for some time and I asked the doctor if I could come off it. He agreed, so long as I wore Ted stockings.

Ted stockings are thick and very, very tight. Very difficult for the nurses to put on. Boy, how they struggled. I think they recommend them on long-haul flights or anywhere where you are sitting down a lot, as again they reduce the risk of thrombosis.

Claudia pulled down my cards and pictures, taking half the paint with them, which I found very amusing. The walls were now bare and covered in big, roundish marks, where Claudia had removed the tack or tape. Claudia had remarked that one poster would cover most or all of the marks. I suggested three.

An Indian rug was put on the wall. It was very bright colours and yes, it hid most of the damage done by Claudia.

I have already said about one patient being partially deaf, there was another that swore a lot. He shouted and shouted out obscenities, really bad ones. How his mother tolerated him, God only knows. She pushed him in his wheelchair while he shouted his demands. He also swore and spoke very loudly in his sleep. One night, at about one when I was awake, he shouted something about his wheels. I just couldn't stop laughing. He shouted out "Bollocks" on another occasion, which I found amusing.

He shouted his demands to the nurses. They just took everything in their stride. I think he had had a motorbike crash.

Another had short-term memory loss. When he was put in his bed at night, he asked for bisc-weet. Then he rang the bell again, because he could not remember having any. Then he rang again and again and again and again, until he eventually went to sleep.

One patient, who had terminal multiple sclerosis, was the life and soul of any party. She was wheelchair bound, but also had a very infectious loud laugh, which you could hear all over the Unit. One constantly tried escaping. She was suicidal.

On two separate nights, we had the hospital radio come in. They played me a request. On both occasions, I chose Glen Miller.

Claudia bought Giona over. God, he had grown. He chatted away, in Italian of course. I caught the odd word, but had to rely on Claudia to translate.

In my last meeting it was put forward that it was time for me to leave the Rowans Rehabilitation Unit, as my progress was slowing down. Torbay hospital was nominated as being the most suitable option. I would enjoy Torbay, my key worker said. They had an immediate vacancy. One week later, on the Friday, early in the morning, I was told I could leave that day at two o'clock. I was packed up. I had accumulated a lot of stuff, which was packed in various bags and boxes, placed on a trolley and left outside what had been my room.

I was very emotional the day I left Rowans. Well, I had been there for some seven months. Did I think I would always be there? I don't know. I was comfortable there and everybody knew me, so somewhere new, although exciting, as they would do things differently, was daunting.

The ambulance came, loaded my things, then me, and I was off. The speech therapist was looking out of the window as the ambulance moved off. I cried. It took about one and a half hours for the ambulance to make its way to its destination.

CHAPTER EIGHT

The ward I was assigned to, George Earl, was very depressing. It was a stroke unit, but full of old people. A nurse unpacked my things. The ward manager told me I would have to send some things home, as it was only a temporary measure, being at the hospital, until I was assessed and discharged and they just did not have the facilities. Not what my key worker had insinuated at Rowans. I was very much under the impression that I would be there for a long time. Thank God I wasn't. As it turned out, I was there for five weeks. Yes, I had my own room, but it was tiny. I could barely fit in, in my wheel chair. When my wheelchair was charged, it was taken into the day room. There was no wardrobe for my clothes, only a small locker. I was unpacked the best way possible. My sister came, along with a friend, and they finished off the unpacking.

I lost control of my bladder there and my trousers were quite often wet, even though I was wearing a conveen. Hospital ones just didn't fit. I was rapidly going through my trousers, even though my sister bought extra pairs in for me.

Eventually, my sister drove down to Rowans and picked up some better fitting conveens and the hospital got hold of some for me that fitted better.

I asked if I could go off the unit, but was told I couldn't until I was assessed. They were afraid I might get disorientated, as they were used to old fogies that would get disorientated, I am sure.

I asked again, later in the week and I was seen off the ward. I think they could see I was different to what they were normally used to.

George Earl ward was situated in a wing of the hospital on the hospital's fifth floor, the fourth floor being the ground floor. I never quite worked it out either.

To get anywhere of any interest meant going in the lift. The nurse called the lift for me and saw me in, as it was my first time. I could easily reach the buttons in the lift. I just sat out the front of the main entrance. You could often find me there, just thinking.

What a life this was. I had been given this and I had to deal with it. There was no way out, no escape. I often contemplated death, but how could I do it?

It was whilst on the George Earl ward that I started to get very depressed and very, very paranoiac, even though I took an antidepressant.

I always went off the ward when I could. I sat outside mostly. Unless it was too cold, then I sat just inside the doors.

Whenever friends or family came to see me, we either stayed in my room, or went to the restaurant, which had big windows and through the day it had a view of the sea.

I regularly sent a text to Claudia, but I was depressed and my text reflected that. I only saw the unhappy side of life. I did not like it . there. I did not like most of the nurses, who were foreign. Even though I used the communication aid, most did not understand it and they regularly got things wrong. One of the most annoying things that started to happen was they would walk away before the Lightwrighter had even finished. You would not just walk away if, you were having a conversation with someone.

Then I was visited by two nurses from Rowans. I sent a text to Claudia that evening to tell her. She got very angry with me. Nothing was meant by it, but because of my behaviour before, she didn't trust me. I tried to phone her, several times, but she just kept hanging up on me. I was very, very upset.

The physiotherapists ordered me a new ankle splint for my left foot, as the splint I had didn't offer enough support. They tried hoisting me up to a standing position on a special hoist that was attached to the ceiling, but I felt like Peter Pan. I thought it was funny and started laughing, uncontrollably. My emotional liability just interfered. Physiotherapy was about the best thing there, even if they didn't have a bike.

I cannot begin to tell you everything that happened there, but I will briefly tell you about some of the incidents.

They regularly got mixed up about the pills you took. My thumb was trapped on the Standaid twice, which bloody hurt, even though I tried to tell them something was wrong. They just ignored me. I told one nurse to permanently disconnect my conveen and was told later that day by another nurse that she herself disconnected it, when all she did was actually take it off. It was silly really, but she did insist she took it off and disconnected it, she caused a big argument. That night I was put to bed like a scolded child and they forgot the call bell. I tried screaming, but the door was shut and no one came. Thank God I had my mobile phone to hand, so I could text my sister and get her to phone them up and tell them. And all because I got so mad with her, well, what was she insinuating? On a number of occasions I was left waiting to go to bed for ages and ages. I am not talking minutes, how about an hour and a half, and all because the nurse I had told had forgotten. One night I was watching TV in my room when a disorientated granny walked in. I tried to tell her it was not her room. I pressed the bell for a nurse, but they never rushed there. She said "See, no one is coming". I began to scream. With that, she began slapping me in the face, knocking my glasses off. I tried to fend her off, but with one arm dead and the other very weak, it was difficult. Eventually a nurse came and took her out. Naturally I was very upset. It's not every day you get attacked by an eighty odd year-old granny!

They just couldn't cope with someone younger, with a normal brain, they just weren't used to it.

I think I stopped needing suction there, for my teeth. I was able to dribble into a cup.

41

Claudia, by this time, was coming over about every four weeks. I should think that it's very tiring to keep coming over. Being a mother must take its toll too. Being loyal to me also, after I had let her down, must have given her something to think about.

I didn't have any puddings at all there, as I noticed I was still putting on weight and the dietician came and had a word with me. I agreed to eat more, as my weight had gone from 72 kilos to 65 kilos in about three weeks.

The thickener there was different. I needed more, three to be precise. It was still thinner than what I was used to at Rowans.

I was tested again, by a speech therapist, on my ability to swallow un-thickened drinks. The therapist decided that I could go onto un-thickened drinks, so long as I took my time and had two swallows. She annotated it on a board above the bed, which the nurses never read.

The food there was okay, nothing to write home about, but I kept forgetting some special oil that my sister got that you had to take with food. It was kept in the fridge. Eventually it was kept in my room, on the table so I wouldn't forget it. I had it every morning, on my biscweet, which I had now progressed on to. The nurses put it on. It was supposed to help rejuvenate the brain cells.

I stopped using the side supports there. I never liked them anyway, because they seemed to squash me.

My mother was admitted with stomach pains. She was put on a nice ward and just for once, I was the visitor. I wended my way through the endless corridors and up lifts, to go and see her. When we could, in the evening, we played "Connect four" or "Four in a row" together. She had fluid in her tummy, which was preventing her from eating. She was very weak.

Whenever I went out, off the ward, I took a bottle with me. My plan was to go to the nearest ward. As it happened, I was never caught short. I was a couple of times when I went visiting my mother. All the nurses knew of me and once I was there and they couldn't get to me in time and I wet myself. I had to go back to my ward to get changed. I hated not being in control of my bladder. It was embarrassing.

The fluid was drained off and sent away for analysis. It took many days to get the result, but when it did come it wasn't good news.

CHAPTER NINE

S he had had cancer some years before. She was told that the fluid was cancerous and she would need to undergo a more rigorous treatment than she had previously had, if she wanted to eliminate it, although there were no guarantees. She was 72 but looked quite a lot younger. As there were no guarantees and she was told the treatment would be painful, she decided not to have it.

Outwardly, she seemed happy. Who knows what goes on inside though?

It was whilst at Torbay that I got a new communication aid. Basically the same, but it didn't have a robotic voice, which the other one had. The keys on it were plastic, as opposed to rubber. It did a few more things, but it looked the same as the old one, which was subsequently taken away and sent back to Rowans. This one was on loan too, from the Speech Therapy Department.

I had an allergic reaction to some medication I was taking for a urine infection. I came out in a very bad rash, which I didn't notice at first. It made me very weak, not just in things I did, but in my speech as well. Prior to that, my speech was getting much better. Still quiet, but much clearer. It still wasn't good, but it was better. The illness knocked me back, it seemed, about four or five months. My speech became non-existent.

I was so weak that even the lift buttons became difficult to press.

My mother was there for about three weeks.

One night whilst she was there, I dropped my glasses. They were nowhere to be found. I asked around several times, but no one handed them in. I would have handed them in — just who would have taken them? They were reading glasses after all. Useful I guess, if you had the same prescription and need glasses for reading, or if you know someone that does. I was able to put them on and take them off by myself. I had put them on my lap, I guess they must have slid off.

It was a shame really that because of my illness my speech was not very good when Claudia came over with Giona.

The food their was okay, but I was given gravy with everything, even scrambled egg.

I ate in my room again. I definitely wasn't going to eat with these oldies.

Breakfast was in bed about 8.30. The domestic staff bought it round. I was supposed to be supervised every mealtime in case I choked, but never was. In fact, I was better at eating on my own, so it was a blessing in disguise.

I complained that I was getting lower back ache. My mattress was changed, which helped a little, but I mainly relied on two paracetamol to help take away the pain.

Claudia bought me some more glasses from a large supermarket. I guessed at the strength I would need. I was right. My mother told my sister to buy me a glasses cord that goes over your neck, so I wouldn't lose them.

Because she had brought Giona, we all went to my mum's ward to visit her. It was quite emotional.

I choked very violently by my mum, one night. I was given half a chocolate honeycombed sweet, thinking I could keep it in my mouth and it would just melt. It didn't. It went straight to the back of my throat, everybody was very worried, including Claudia. I had nurses on standby with suction. I calmed down a bit and just sat quietly.

Claudia took me on my first outing, which was the seafront. She ordered a wheelchair taxi, which is like a London black cab. He dropped us at one end of the seafront and met us about an hour later at the other. It wasn't far and we walked slowly, as Jacob and Giona were with us. We stopped for ice cream, a small tub for me that Claudia fed me and a cone for every one else.

When my mother was discharged, I didn't know what to do, or where to go. Just stay out of that ward. I was always out, afternoons and as late as possible in the evenings. I only ate and slept in that place, so I didn't do any writing there. I went outside, or just went exploring around the hospital, until about eleven o'clock, when I went back.

One night, whilst exploring, I got shut between two doors, I could only go forward or back about twenty meters. The doors closed automatically, they were closed against me, I needed to pull them, I was stuck. As luck would have it, someone came along and let me out. There were no more doors to negotiate.

I developed a taste for chocolate buttons and, to prove my independence to myself, I went into the hospital shop and asked for some. Could they be opened, placed on my lap and could the shop assistant help themselves to the money, which was attached, by string, to my wheelchair. All that with my communication aid. I was not afraid to use it to ask for things. One day I had white ones as well. I stopped . just below the ward, turned my wheelchair so it was facing the window and ceremoniously ate them.

It was whilst at the hospital that I discovered I was very jumpy. A nurse briskly came into my room one breakfast time when I was drinking coffee and scared me. It went everywhere.

It was agreed that I could visit two places and decide where my next move would be. My sister came to both places to help me decide.

My first visit was to a care home in Paignton, Devon, for about 27 people. My description of it on my mobile was: "… it's like an old hotel…" which it is. It is very creaky with narrow corridors. I immediately liked it. You could see the sea from the lounge and could easily access it.

I then went to a care home in Brixham, Devon. I didn't like it much, it was purpose built and it seemed very institutionalised. Both would take me around the 20th of December. It was early December when I visited them and I stayed for lunch. I was a bit nervous about eating with other people, I was okay though. At Paignton it was cottage pie, which was very nice, in Brixham, the next day, it was fish and chips. Part of the care home in Brixham did overlook a small cove, but I could not see a way down to it. I doubt it was wheelchair accessible anyway. I had made my decision.

During my last few days there, I was moved out of my room and onto the ward, which I didn't really mind, as I was counting the days.

Once again my things were packed into boxes and bags. I was informed that the ambulance crew would only take an essentials bag and the hospital notes. So I had to ask my sister and some friends to take some things. I said goodbye to the staff I liked. Yes, there were some nice staff there.

I was not emotional when I left.

CHAPTER TEN

I t's very difficult when one day I was windsurfing, driving etc, doing normal things that we take for granted, then, wham! Then you need help even going to the toilet. It doesn't creep up on you, like an illness. It gives you no time to prepare. Maybe I was stressed, but I had no indicators that I was. My blood pressure seemed okay. How long will I be disabled now? Forever? The worst thing was that my brain still seemed to function normally. It's just my body and bodily functions that don't work.

I was given room fourteen at Oldway Heights. There was an upstairs, which was accessible by a lift that kept breaking down, but I was to be downstairs. Oldway was halfway up a hill. The room was sort of in between the dining room and nurses' station, so they could keep an eye on me. It was light pink (mmmm, that's nice) and about eight foot by fourteen foot, with a sink and en-suite toilet. It had windows that looked out on the driveway and in the distance I could see the sea. It had a wardrobe, a chest of drawers and a dressing table just inside on the left, behind the door, oh and a bed on the right, which you could just get round. Each room had a call bell facility, accessible on the wall and, if necessary, a wire and handheld bell push. My left hand was dexterous enough to use one of these. A carer, for that's what they were called there, unpacked one box. I kept two packed as I was told this was only a temporary room. Claudia wasn't with me this time either.

It was just before Christmas 2004 and they were having their Christmas party. I sat at the back of the lounge, while the rest of the residents joined in with the festive fun. I was given some punch. I tried to drink it, but found it very difficult, my lability got in the way. I needed to concentrate, but it was difficult with the party going on, so I went back to my room and my drink was placed on the table that was in there. I managed two glasses. I could overcome my lability if I was on my own.

They were having a buffet and I thought it was best if I ate in my room, so my first meal, lunch, was mashed potato and beans. I ate in the dining room at teatime, although drinking was a little difficult, but I managed. Normally mealtimes were breakfast from eight thirty to about ten, lunch at twelve thirty and tea at five. Because I couldn't fit under the main table, I was given an extension table. Apart from my visit there, that was the first time I ate with other people.

The bed didn't incline as it did at Rowans or at Torbay, but it was comfortable.

The next day I asked if I could go down to the town, to buy Christmas presents. I was told I could, but someone would have to go with me to make sure I was safe. It was further than I thought. There were some local shops, but none had what I wanted. Because the wheelchair was slow, it took about one hour to get to the town. I guess it would take an able-bodied person about half an hour to cover the same distance. I did my Christmas shopping, which was fun, as I just pointed to the things I wanted and the carer that came with me picked the items up. They were wrapped later and I told a carer, who wrapped them up for me, what to write on them. Two days later, which was Christmas Eve, I needed to go again. Again the Manager told me I could, if I had someone with me. I argued about having someone go with me, because I wanted to be independent. I guess at Torbay there was an element of safety and I spent most of my time inside, where there was no traffic. They were only looking out for my safety. I eventually reluctantly agreed and made my way to the town.

I stayed in most of Christmas day, but I did have some visitors on Christmas day morning, including Jacob.

I had hidden his present under the bed and when he slid it out, he eagerly opened it. He was delighted when he ripped the paper off and found an electric racing car set, as unbeknown to me it was one of the things on his wish list.

I had Christmas lunch in the dining room with the rest of the residents that were there, for some had gone away. I didn't have long to wait after my two coffees before the taxi came. I was going for tea to a friend's parents house. I had ordered the wheelchair taxi some days before. It didn't take long and I was there.

I tried a drink, but my lability was just too much. I could eat okay in front of people, but couldn't drink, so I refused all drinks. Maybe that's why I didn't have a wee all the time I was there.

We ate buffet-style, in the kitchen. All that were there, including two children, treated me like Tim, not disabled Tim, but plain old Tim.

I don't know what I was expecting, sympathy I suppose, but they just got on with things and I wasn't treated any differently.

The next day, Boxing Day, I went to visit my mother for tea by taxi. It was difficult to gain access into my mother's bungalow. It involved going in next door's drive, whom I presumed they had consulted before my arrival (I found out later, that they hadn't), four planks of wood of various sizes and going through some bushes to get in. Once in, I was okay. My sister was there, with her family. We watched television, ate and then we all played some games, before it was time for me to go. I managed a little vodka with pineapple juice, but I was quite surprised at how overpowering the taste was. It reminded me of the first time I ever tried alcohol.

I forgot my wee bottle, so, imagine the scene: me and my sister out in the hallway with me weeing in an orange bottle, just because it had a wide neck and my sister holding the bottle down. Needless to say, I found the whole thing very amusing and didn't wee much.

Getting out was just a reversal of getting in, with my mother looking on anxiously and shouting out instructions.

It was quite expensive to go to my mother's, well Paignton to Teignmouth is quite a way, but I didn't mind.

Christmas came and went. I guess I was looking forward to Claudia coming over, just before the New Year.

I went shopping again, this time for Claudia and Giona and myself. I bought a rain cover that not only covered me, but went over the entire chair as well. I must have looked silly in it, but it was practical in the rain, if ever I was caught out, or if I had to go out, like to the doctors, which was just down the road. I also bought a rucksack that went over the back of the chair. I bought Giona a train he could push around on the floor and an automated train set that changed and picked up boulders, continuously. He liked trains. There were trains on both sides of the flat in Rome, the main intercity line directly out the back and some sidings across the road, out the front. He couldn't help but like them. I bought Claudia some walking boots.

Claudia came with Giona and I was very emotional. I was always very emotional whenever she came and went. Just the thought of her coming and I would get very emotional. Mainly I would cry.

We all decided to go out on New Year's Eve, so we went to a famous pizza restaurant. This was a big thing for me, as it was the first time I had eaten out and I was afraid I might get labile and cause a scene. I wasn't, of course. I didn't have a drink though. I didn't make a mess with my food. I chose lasagne and the whole evening went very well and the taxi soon arrived back to pick us up. Jacob was collected at the care home by his mum. We finished off the evening, in the dark, outside with a glass of champagne, of which I managed a sip. Giona had some as well, only a little. He liked it and asked for more.

Jacob was with us and we all went to a friend's wedding and wedding reception. It was miles away in mid-Devon and a taxi was hired for the day. We didn't pay, the happy couple did.

The taxi arrived for one o'clock and it took just over an hour to get there. We quickly stopped just by the church, for me to have a wee, in the taxi of all places. Claudia looked stunning; she didn't often wear makeup except some eye liner, but when she did. . . . . Wow!

I wore a suit I had bought some years before. We made our way to the reception.

When we got there, Claudia removed the armrests from my chair, so I could fit under the table and slowly guided me in. I ate, but declined all drinks, just in case I was labile. I didn't need another wee. We left just after the speeches at about eight. we had been out for a long time.

Again, we all went to the cinema, which was a disaster. We had planned to walk there, but, because it was spitting with rain when we went out, Claudia tried to book a taxi – to no avail as it was too late. This ate into our walking time and we were very late. I ran over Giona's foot. It didn't help that I laughed about the situation. I just couldn't help it. It was a bad effect of my lability. Then my wheelchair was switched off at the crossing we were supposed to cross at, first by Claudia, because she wanted to cross and get some fish and chips, then when I switched it on again, Jacob switched it off. I got very frustrated and upset and screamed because I was prevented from switching my wheelchair on by Jacob. This in turn got Jacob upset. Eventually Claudia understood that we needed to cross, I saw the traffic lights were at red but the little man was not at green, but I still crossed the road when a car was coming, Claudia shouted at me, even though I knew it was relatively safe to cross. We all arrived at the cinema, late, but we still went in.

I was angry with myself for getting upset. About the only thing I could control, the wheelchair, was switched off and I was prevented from switching it on. The wheelchair made me slightly independent and for someone else to take control of my independence was too much.

We went to the seafront while Claudia and Giona were over. I wasn't that cold even though it was winter. I wore a fleece over a t-shirt, but Claudia insisted that I wear hat, gloves and a scarf. It was cold to her. I rarely felt the cold, only in my fingers, where I chronically suffered from Raynaud's phenomenon (a narrowing of arteries and capillaries in cold weather).

What got me was the children's acceptance. To them it didn't matter that Dad was disabled, even Giona looked at me with respect. Jacob seemed to understand nearly everything I said, which I think is amazing. Although Giona spoke in Italian and I could see he loved and respected Claudia, I have to say that Claudia is a fantastic mother. She even gets Jacob's respect.

Most evenings Claudia did the catering and we ate in the dining room, as a family.

Unfortunately it soon came to Claudia and Giona going. I was very emotional, as usual.

CHAPTER ELEVEN

I soon got used to life at Oldway Heights. My improvement was very slow now.

I had my own DVD player, which, previously, I had the nurses put the discs in. I don't know why, but I wanted to see if I could put the discs in now and I could. One more thing on the road to independence. I had also stopped using the possum that I bought with me from Rowans, which was on loan, for as long as I needed it. Conventional controls, although difficult, were adequate for me now. Books were hard though, although I had a reading stand. I found it impossible to turn the pages without them flipping back, so I gave up.

A suggestion was that I get an electric rotary shaver, as it would give me something to aim for. So I drove off to the local electrical shop, with a carer, to buy a shaver. By the next week I was using it quite successfully.

It was suggested that I meet another stroke victim. She could just walk, but spent most of her time in an electric wheelchair. She was completely paralysed when she first came to Oldway, from what I understand, some two years ago, but I don't think her stroke was not as severe as mine. I had noticed that her right arm was completely useless. I had some movement in mine. Her left arm, moved normally, from what I could see. A similar age to me, she was very jovial, I had some questions for her, obviously. What were the questions? That's a secret. I understood most of what she said, even though she couldn't speak.

At Christmas I got an amaryllis (that's a plant to those of you who don't know). I watched it grow and grow from a bulb. I had been given plants as presents before, some had died, but now I had a bee in my bonnet that I must soon go to a flower shop. The day I bought the razor, I also went to a flower shop. I bought a cyclamen and some lilies. The cyclamen subsequently died, but it looked nice while it lasted.

I was weeing quite successfully into the bottle. They had plastic ones there that were rinsed out, with water, after use. They still had to place it, which meant that the carer that answered my bell had to undo my zip and help me out. I got wet on occasions and I screamed if I had to hold on, but most of the time I was okay. Mornings went well, but I found afternoons and evenings tricky for controlling my bladder.

My scalp still itched and the sensation would cause me to jump so much that my feet would quite often become displaced on the foot rests on my wheelchair. It was mainly first thing in the morning, when my hair was brushed, but also at night, when I was on the computer, which was most evenings. I would block my feet on a chest of drawers when I was on the computer so they couldn't come off the footplates, which was quite successful.

When I was at Rowans, back in November, I was measured for a tray, which was to be fitted to my wheelchair. It was designed so it would slide on and off my chair, as I needed it, by a metal tube that was fixed to my chair. It took bloody ages to come through. I eventually got the tray when I was at Oldway Heights, in February. Prior to that, I asked for my laptop to be placed on my room table, which was used for drinks mainly, food as well at Rowans.

My wheelchair broke on a number of occasions. Not down to my driving, I might add. Just due to everyday wear and tear. The legs kept dropping down, about one inch, all due to a silly little bolt that stopped the leg from swinging out to the side. I am sure the temporary repairs were stronger.

The carers worked a variation of different shifts, eight in the morning till two, two till five, five till eight, five till eleven and there was the night crew, two of them, who worked eight at night till eight in the morning, so there was someone always there. They worked hard and enjoyed their job. There were mostly six on two shifts through the day and two at night, so there were quite a few of them. They were very friendly towards you, but also gave you your own space.

They would get you up between just gone eight and nine o'clock. I needed non-slip mats in the morning, as that's the time I was weakest. If they tried to use the Standaid without mats, my right foot would uncontrollably slip back, leaving me on one leg and I would scream.

I was showered twice a week, on a Monday and a Friday, on all the other days I got a bed bath each morning. I would have a wet shave on a Friday, as I was allergic to electric shaving and it gave me a rash on my neck if I used it all the time. This had always been the case, since I started shaving. I verbally chose my own clothes, which they understood. I didn't bother with underpants or boxers, as I just couldn't see the point, it was one more piece of fiddly clothing I could easily do without. Then, when I was dressed and in my chair, my communication aid and phone, which were on a board, were placed on my knee. Then there were the cleaners, the activity organisers, the kitchen staff, the laundry staff, the driver-cum- maintenance man, the Manager, the lady that kept the accounts, the lady that came in to do the wages and the owner. He drove a variety of cars and came in most days. He also owned a rest home for the elderly and on top of a Chrysler Voyager with a personalized number plate, he also owned a silver Maserati with a personalized number plate. Bastard. I guess the care industry paid well.

When it was shower day, I was ceremoniously wheeled in a purpose-made shower chair to the shower, which was either upstairs or down. Downstairs was only lukewarm, which I got used to. As it was very temperamental, I would be taken upstairs, if it was too cold. I had a sheet wrapped round me to preserve my dignity. My feet would often drag, so I went backwards. When we got there, the carers showered me, paying particular attention to my feet. I am sure it was because I was ticklish there. I screamed loudly when my feet were washed, much to the amusement of the carers. When they were finished, I was wheeled back and dressed.

Why do some people talk to you loud and deliberate? *Good . . . Morning . . . Tim . . . How. . . are . . . you?* Or they talk to you with raised voices, as if I am a child or a pussy cat. I am not deaf or stupid. It happened at Rowans, it happened at Torbay, now here. Not everybody, I might add, just the few. The majority were okay and they spoke to you normally. People talk over you, as well: they talk to each other, as if you're not there. "What does Tim like to wear?" "Does Tim like it this way?". Why don't they bloody ask me? I can speak, sort of, or I can speak through the communication aid.

It's funny, we all hear of writers getting blocked, well, it's true. It happened to me on many occasions. When I didn't have access to my laptop, as it was put away, when I didn't use it, I knew what I wanted to write, but when I had my laptop, I quite often became blocked.

I went out, I think it was to the doctors, which was in the next road and I made a mental note of a florist that we passed.

I started to buy more plants for my room, from the local florist. First it was three spider plants, for the three shelves I had put up, then it was three peace lilies, then a rubber plant, then a ficus benjamina, then a draconea, not all at the same time, over a few weeks. They delivered them. Plus the plants and flowers I already had, or were bought in by subsequent visitors. I was mad for plants. Walking into my room was like walking into a flower shop or Kew Gardens.

My room was very cold. I didn't have the radiator on, I liked it that way. I didn't really feel the cold, so my window was always open a little bit, except when Claudia was over. She always thought, England was very cold and closed my window. When I was in Rome, I loved the heat and dressed accordingly. I was a sun worshiper. I didn't lie in it, but I did take my shirt off whenever I could.

I also bought an electric toothbrush, from the same shop I bought the shaver from. I had been bought an electric toothbrush before, but I couldn't switch it on or off and it was too big for my mouth. I didn't know it at the time that it was too big, I just struggled with it. I got the carers to clean them at first, as I found it hard to lift my left elbow. The new one was easier to turn on and off and it was slightly smaller, so anybody that insinuates that I have a big mouth, they're wrong, I have the proof.

I didn't really need to spit, as most of the toothpaste fell out my mouth anyway. The same as eating, I had to make sure I swallowed it, or it would fall out, on the next fork full.

I was okay at eating and drinking, as I tended to rest my left elbow on the armrest of the wheelchair.

I was promised a bigger room, when one became available, by the Manager, as it was a bit small for me in there.

Physiotherapy was supplied at Oldway, but only once a week and lasted about forty to fifty minutes, or less. Gosh, my legs were so tight in the mornings and the physiotherapist struggled with them. I was promised more from Torbay, but they hadn't been yet. After all, it was only February. Why the wait, you might ask. The answer is I don't know. I was told by the physiotherapist at Oldway that I could do with physiotherapy every day and recommended that I didn't stay in the wheelchair all day. So, I went on the bed most afternoons and watched a DVD or video, then got up again for tea about half four. Although that petered off, as I would prefer to work on my laptop. I liked being creative, or surfing the net.

I decided that I would benefit from a massage once a week. The home already supplied a masseuse on a weekly basis, but that was for about twenty minutes. I asked her if she would take me on, for an hour each week. Privately. I guess she must have been desperate or something, because she agreed to take me on.

One year on and I still ask myself the same question: why me? A stroke, such as mine, is a devastating thing. It not only affects you, by taking your life away, but, to some extent, affects everyone around you. Will I ever get used to it? I don't know. Yes, I will adapt to it, but I will always show some signs of it. It's a cruel, cruel thing. I am sure dying is easier all round, maybe that's me, just being selfish. I want my

58

life back. I keep waking up, hoping this is a bad dream, or I wake up hoping I can talk again. My mind is still the same, so it seems that's what makes it crueller. I can't see any light at the end of the tunnel. People keep telling me I will improve, but to what extent? What do they know anyway? Each stroke is as individual as you or I. Am I bitter? Yes, I bloody well am!

Even though I didn't use it, it was easier for me to have the headrest back on, in case it was lost. Anyway, I was grateful for it in the summer, when I was to sunbathe. Whenever Jacob came to visit, which was about once a week, without Claudia and Giona, he would stay about one hour and was dropped off by his mum and then she would come back later and pick him up. We did homework. I was able to be a Dad again, advising him what the correct answers would be, by me speaking which he understood, or by me using the communication aid. After we had finished, he put on one of the CDs he had brought and dance for me and I would nod my head. It was so funny and we would laugh.

I was sure I was still putting on weight, I didn't need to weigh myself. My trousers didn't fit. It was a shock, I was so used to being slim. Just under a thirty inch waist, is what I was used to. I guess I had gone up to a thirty-three inch waist. My trousers previously had no flies and had an elasticised waist, so I didn't *really* notice I was putting on weight, but now I started to wear ordinary trousers. There is no way you could do up the top button, but that was okay, as you couldn't see it, as I wore my t-shirt outside of my trousers. I suppose, leading a sedentary lifestyle, it was easy to put on weight.

At Rowans I went on the exercise bike, which I guess helped a bit, now I didn't do anything.

I put myself on a diet, only eating half of what was put in front of me, except cheesecake. I loved that and ate it all up and my breakfast. I loved my food, but, thank goodness, my narcissistic willpower was stronger than my liking for food. I cut down on my sugar intake. Instead of two sugars, I went down to one and I cut back on the amount of coffee I drank. I was used to drinking six now, two at each mealtime, so I only had three. I did read somewhere that post-stroke people should avoid caffeine, but I didn't heed that warning. I liked my coffee black. I replaced my coffee with a mix of two juices, which I was already having, orange and cranberry.

My aim was to get down to a comfortable, thirty-two inch waist. Previously, I had been a thirty inch waist, or just under. I was very slim and took care of my appearance. I went to the gym, most nights, when I was in England.

One of the carers constantly teased me about my diet. I told her I liked cheesecake. Big mistake. The next time cheesecake was on the menu, she gave me such a big piece. I couldn't eat it though, because of my lability. I laughed and the carers gathered round me. I was getting so distressed, I eventually left it and my coffee. I fled back to my room.

Once I was in the dining room and the two ladies that sat opposite me (who you will read about in the next chapter) began talking. They were so funny, everybody could clearly hear what they were saying. They were so serious, as they talked about rubbish. I laughed so much and kept laughing, the sandwich that I was eating fell out my mouth. I couldn't eat any more, they were so funny though.

I asked my sister to buy me some new trousers, this time with a thirty-two inch waist. I could barely do them up. And a dressing gown, as I didn't have one. My elasticised waist trousers, although nice, were put in the bottom of the wardrobe. I eventually had six pairs of casual, thirty-two inch waist trousers, two of which were lost by the laundry lady, for a very long time.

I still kept eating my stash of chocolate in my room though. I had a liking for not only chocolate buttons, but chocolate fingers as well. My mother introduced me to wafer-thin chocolate mints. She kept all my chocolate supplies topped up, as did Claudia.

It was difficult to follow my diet when Claudia was over, as we always ate so well. So I was only dieting when Claudia went back to Rome. She didn't think I was fat.

CHAPTER TWELVE

I kept myself to myself there. Well, it is difficult mixing, when you have lost the power of speech. You feel alone, isolated. I only ventured out of my room at mealtimes or when I needed to see the Manager. The residents regularly went out on trips and there were activities, from bingo and quizzes to making glittery boxes and toilet rolls that could be turned into something useful, and painting. Riveting stuff. They also regularly had entertainment come in, which was in the residents' lounge along with the daily activities. I didn't participate in any of those (I wonder why). Mixing, along with being awkward, was something I didn't like to do as it made me feel more disabled. I liked my own company anyway.

I have to say, mealtimes were very entertaining. It was the place to be if you liked nonsense. We all made our way into the dining room at mealtimes and sat at our designated places. There was one resident who mumbled to herself, another who had also suffered a stroke, she laughed a lot and couldn't really speak, except to say "Oh dear", which she said perfectly. One elderly chap, who had Parkinson's and who slowly came in, in his electric wheelchair, still managed to crash though, even if he was going at a snail's pace, taking half the dining room with him. He was constantly falling asleep, in the dining room, in a position where you would think he would fall out of his wheelchair. There was one who, when he had finished, tried to stand up on his own. He wasn't allowed to, in case he fell over. Later he was allocated a wheelchair, but still tried to escape by pulling himself along with his feet. One who laughed so much she was sick on occasions and was violent, she was rushed out by the carers. Her violent spells got worse and the home couldn't offer her the one to one, twenty-four hour care she needed, so she was sent to a more specialised unit, which I guess was more geared up for her condition. She was only young, in her twenties, but had the demeanour of somebody much, much younger most of the time. One who constantly kicked the table and screamed when things didn't go her way (which come to think of it, was practically all the time). One who was blind and who constantly moaned. He could just stand but was mostly taken everywhere in a wheelchair and was wheeled off to bed, straight after tea. A lady who got very, very stroppy, especially if she had to repeat everything, which the carers made her do, just to wind her up. She cleaned and dusted everything before she started eating and did a funny ritual with her Zimmer frame, along with "dusting" the air high in front of her, quite regularly. I must admit, the first time she did it, I thought she was waving to someone, I didn't know she was as mad as a hatter. She was quite often falling asleep in the lounge and when she was woken up, just before mealtime, she would swear blind, she had just had her meal. I wonder what she was dreaming about. Or she would say that it wasn't mealtime yet. One gentleman who kept having to be reminded about pudding. One old chap, who was very tall and gangly and quite often wore trousers that had had an argument with his ankles and a jacket that didn't meet his wrists, he constantly hovered when it was close to drinks time. One morning, when I was eating breakfast late, he must have come in the dining room about twenty times, looking for the tea trolley. He must have had a very short-term memory. There was another middle-aged chap who forever kept going on about the pain he was in – which I am sure he was. You could hear him coming as he constantly went on about the pain he was in and moaned and groaned his way around the building. I do wonder if when he is in his room, he goes on about his pain then, when no one can hear him. He made very droll remarks, when he was at the dinner table, along with laughing at his own jokes, which weren't even funny and burping a lot. He made these droll comments a lot, in everyone else's conversation.

He complimented everybody with silly comments and talked to everybody as if they were much younger than him, or like they were a pet dog like "Good boy" or "Good lad" or "Good girl". I got the impression that no one really liked him, residents and carers alike. I know I didn't.

He said he was on a diet, but he ate all his food and he quite often asked for more. I don't know why, but he also called me Paul, as he said it suited me and was for ever changing his career. He was quite mad.

There was one man, who had a three-wheeled folding walker that squeaked. You could hear the squeak before you could see him. He was eventually oiled.

Then there was a new lady who would put her teeth in, which she carried with her, before every mealtime. Then, when she was finished, she took them back out again and put them away in their tooth case. Later she was very chuffed, as she got a new, see-through case, so you could see her gnashers now. Lovely. Thank God she favoured the other one. Why would you want to see them anyway? She was forever knocking her walking stick over, or she would put it at a precarious angle, so the carers that were serving would kick it over. It clattered on the floor and I would jump. She also cried when she spoke, even when ordering her breakfast. She had had a stroke. She would give you a running commentary on who had walked past the dining room and kitchen doors.

Squeaky and Gummy became more than great friends, going everywhere together, going on personal appointments together, arriving and leaving the dining room together, sitting together, spending the day together, going to each other's rooms, holding hands to comfort each other. They were like an old married couple that were still very much in love, talking about things that didn't matter. Not that all old couples talk about things that are insignificant mind, they did. They were constantly asking if the other one was okay, "Are you alright?". it happened about twice each, each mealtime, so say they sat eating for about forty-five minutes and they spent each waking moment of the day together, say sixteen hours, that's over eighty-five times in a day one of them says "Are you alright?". For a while, Squeaky's thumb nails were so long, I joked with one of the Senior carers, that his thumbs were auditioning for the part of Fu Manchu. And when he had a hair cut, boy did he have a haircut! Practically as bald as a coot he was. Squeaky always said to one of the carers that was working "I've had some lovely food today" or "I've really enjoyed my food today" – every bloody teatime. They were always late for their meals, they knew they were late and apologized profusely. Why be late then? They didn't have to catch a train or get held up by traffic, no, they were just upstairs. Was the carpet up and they had to do a diversion, was that their excuse? There was nothing in their friendship, at least I don't think so, but who knows what goes on behind closed doors. I am sure they were just close friends, at least I think so.

I didn't know what was wrong with everybody, only the few.

About twenty-two of us ate in the dining room, some of the residents choosing to stay in their rooms.

By far though the most entertaining were the two ladies that sat opposite me, on another table. One when she spoke, spoke very dramatically and frantically, I don't know why but she did. Every time she opened her mouth, she would dramatise everything and told a story, with everything that she said, putting on voices. She was full of useless information and she gestured with her hands. She was registered blind, but could just see and also suffered from multiple sclerosis. The other lady that sat with her listened intently as she spouted out her intense, dramatic drivel. Her voice just irritated the hell out of me. She was in a push wheelchair, which she controlled. She constantly kept going on about wanting anything chocolaty for pudding.

She was slim and could eat anything. Maybe all her gesturing and frantic, dramatic talk kept her slim. The other was the best, she was mid-fifties and kept me constantly entertained with her endless conversations.

You see, due to a heart attack she had a short-term memory problem (obviously, sitting next to frantic, talking-crap lady) and she seemed very simple. She forgot most days that she lived there and kept asking the other lady to confirm it and why she was there, not forgetting her name, thank goodness, or every mealtime we would get "Do I know you?". They were very well suited really, as she would forget what inane drivel she would listen to every mealtime. Perhaps the other lady had a short-term memory problem as well. Either way, she was very patient with her. It would drive me up the wall, always being asked the same thing over and over again. She constantly arrived a few minutes late, no doubt she forgot it was mealtime.

She kept asking the other lady if she could see anything at all. She once asked the other lady, in her simplistic way, "Did you have a mother?". She was very serious when she said it. There was one man on her table who had obviously had enough of her. He constantly ridiculed her, when he got the chance.

One day she was commenting on a brain scan saying "I don't think I've had one of those". As quick as a flash the man said "They would have trouble finding yours, it's so small". She just simply said "Thank you" and carried on eating. It didn't seem to register with her that she had just been insulted.

The other lady kept reminding her to get a pencil and paper to write everything down and have a sticky label put on her, saying she had short-term memory. She forgot, of course. She had no recollection of being taken out by her husband. She was missing at some mealtimes and I overheard the staff saying she was out.

God knows how she knew which seat to sit in, or if she ever found her room. The mind conjures up all sorts of things. Did she watch any repeats on television, did she know they were repeats? Did she recognise her husband? How?

It's funny she remembered every one's name, but couldn't remember if she lived there or what was wrong with her. She had no tact. She once asked a lady "Why are you so fat?". She wasn't exactly slim herself and she said to a young thirteen year-old girl, who was just helping "You haven't got any breasts, what age will you be when you get some?". Needless to say, the young girl was flushed with embarrassment and didn't really answer her. One day, she had visitors come in the dining room briefly at teatime, she eagerly greeted them as it transpired she hadn't seen them for years (she knew that), then asked them "This is real, isn't it?", referring to the home, she then hugged them some more, then asked them "Is this real?". The visitors went out the dining room to wait for her, in some comfy chairs, while she finished her tea. Five minutes later, she asked talking-crap lady "Is this real?". Thinking about it, I guess it must be a nightmare, waking up every day and not knowing why you're there, but as an onlooker, who cares, she was so funny. She was very kind, always helping the other residents where she could. One mealtime, she even did the washing up.

It was the look on her face though. She was so serious as she asked the same questions, over and over again. I liked her though. She cried a lot, when she realised she lived there, which was most days, obviously.

One phrase I hated that was said by some residents to other residents was "Bye, take care". They would see them next mealtime and they didn't go out, so what could happen to them? Would they get mugged by the carers or another resident, or dive in front of the tea trolley and get run over, or get hoovered up by the vacuum cleaner?

What a bunch we were, what with me constantly coughing and choking and all the other residents. Christmas parties for the staff must have been full of conversation about us and our idiosyncrasies.

I guess though I was one of the few lucky ones. My condition was likely to improve, most of them would slowly deteriorate.

Breakfasts were odd. The chef, who was mainly on, liked heavy metal and he would play it while he worked, it filtered out of the serving hatch and mixed with the music on the radio that was always on low on each morning in the dining room.

Breakfasts were from eight thirty-ish, till the last person was finished. Most of the time, I have to say, it was me and sometimes it was nearly ten thirty. At lunchtimes and teatimes they played a CD and it was an opportunity for all the carers (they all served) to act silly and generally entertain you.

I jumped at most things, high-pitched noises mainly. The dining room became a war zone for me.

When knifes and forks were dropped, or when the cutlery was put into its tray, or when crockery was dropped, or someone coughed abruptly, or when another resident dropped their walking stick, when chairs were scraped on the wooden floor, I jumped. Inevitably, I was holding a drink at the time and it would go all over me, upsetting me. I had an apron on to protect me, but it still managed to find its way on to my trousers and t-shirt, somehow.

Even when I went out and a car misfired or honked its horn or when a lorry went past and its air brakes went off. If someone abruptly walked in my room, when the door was shut and they forgot to knock, or even if they did knock, I would jump. Needless to say, I was very nervous when I had a drink and yes, jumping was a problem. Now I know how pets feel when fireworks are set off!

CHAPTER THIRTEEN

A part from the residents, Oldway also had facilities for respite and day care. One of the day care residents was so funny. I guess he was about mid-fifties, a big man that was wheelchair bound. He couldn't speak. He would stab the carers up the bum with his fork and flick their aprons up as they went past. He was a nightmare!

There was one lady that came in on day care, she was so funny. She was in a wheelchair and said "Ow" each time she was moved and she would repeat the last line of a conversation she heard or the last line of a lyric that was played, as if it was a question, which was very confusing for people walking past her, as they just didn't know what she was on about. Her favourite sayings were "That's all right in it" or "That's not nice" or variations thereof. The carers had a ball with her. She was fed, as she would fall asleep or just forget to eat.

We had a virus at Oldway, Norwalk. For a few days we completely closed down, no one in and no one out. The unaffected care workers came in though, they had to wear aprons, gloves and overshoes with every resident, then discard them and start again, so they didn't spread the virus.

We were all asked to stay in our rooms. It didn't really affect me, I did have a temperature one night, but by the morning it had gone. We were allowed out of our rooms, the ones that were well enough that is. The rest of the building seemed like a ghost town, with no one around. I guess the virus had affected most of the residents. After a couple of days of being stuck in my room to eat, I was allowed into the desolate dining room and one by one, day by day, the residents slowly crept back in. All in all, the whole thing lasted about two weeks.

Throughout this time, the carers that came in (as the virus affected some of them as well) certainly earned their money. At mealtimes they delivered the food and drink on a tray to each resident.

My room was a haven for me. I would quite often sit with my laptop on my tray, playing my computer games, or writing, till the early hours of the morning and I would quite often press the call bell, for the elderly chap that lived next door. If you remember, he had a wheelchair and if you ever went past his room, you would see him asleep, in the most precarious of positions. He quite often fell and that's why I would ring the nurse call bell for him. I would hear a thud or his muffled cries for help "Him again".

I had thought about getting an exercise bike, like the one I used at Rowans, for some time. I had even priced them up, whilst I was at Torbay, but now I had my own room. They were about three and a half thousand pounds, but I thought it was a good investment. I would buy it, then, through something my social worker said. I texted my brother and got him to contact the Royal Air Force Benevolent Fund. I had done about five years in the R.A.F.

As my brother was abroad in Cyprus and they would only talk to someone over here, my sister took up the challenge.

I was interviewed by their local representative, who was a retired Warrant Officer, a nice chap and they eventually agreed to buy it outright. I thought they would give me a donation. It would take about six weeks.

It was my idea to ask the Manager if I could have that room as my permanent room. I was sure my bike would fit in it, besides, I liked that room, even if it was a bit noisy with carers constantly walking past and the noisy neighbours. One of them had his television on so loud and carers walking past would turn it down, but he would only turn it up again a few minutes later. Doors were kept open by a special system that would shut automatically if the fire alarm went off.

My speech was much more intelligible now, with most staff being able to understand what I said. Although I was very quiet, I found it was easier to give one or two word answers and any long sentences would be when I used the communication aid, although I did attempt some sentences verbally. I didn't need to recline anymore. My dribbling had greatly improved. I used to dribble such a lot, now I hardly dribble at all. I still dribble a little bit, but I used to have such a problem. My lability still catches me out and I laugh and dribble or I spray saliva all over the carers, when I use the Standaid.

I couldn't walk or talk properly, I had little movement in my left leg and even less in my right. Was I getting more movement back? I suppose I was, but it was painfully slow and insignificant. When I ate or drank or reached for anything, I did it very slowly. I was always one of the last to finish my meals because of this.

I sat on the toilet twice daily, once in the morning and once at night, of which most of the time it was wind, as I couldn't tell the difference. I used the Standaid that they had in the home. After I had been to the toilet, the carers who put me back in my chair took off the support strap and made me lower myself and pull myself up a few times. At that time I couldn't quite lower myself into the wheelchair, but I eventually did. I lowered myself all the way down and then stood up. I found it much harder to stand up if the Standaid was lowered, which they did. Until it was pointed out that they should always use the strap, as it was contravening heath and safety regulations without it. It was making me stronger, but I could see their point, so I reluctantly agreed.

It was whilst on the toilet that I noticed my right upper leg, my thigh, was about two inches shorter than my left. Was it as a result of my strokes? Nobody seemed to know. If it was like it before, surely, I would have noticed. My knees seemed the same height, so, it was just my upper leg. I know muscles can shorten, due to lack of movement, but this seemed to be my bone. As I said, no professional had an answer. Due to the strokes, my hips were not straight and this was likely to be the cause.

71

I had a social worker who had come to see me at Rowans. She was constantly going on holiday, or had days off. I told her that I wanted to be independent. (What was her actual job?). That was one of the biggest things for me.

I was very close to the seafront and I longed to be able to go down there on my own, without any restrictions and just sit there.

I had been assessed by the people that supplied the wheelchair, with regard to my ability and as far as I know, I passed, but I still required a carer to go out with me.

I don't know why, but all my allowances were taking ages to come through. I still didn't get any yet. What does a social worker do? She promised to sort them out, but they were still slow in coming through.

I discovered that I was able to get myself back in the wheelchair. I achieved this by first putting the chair on maximum tilt, then on maximum recline, blocking my feet, then pushing on the arm of the chair with my good arm, the left.

To this day, I don't know why some people get an electric wheelchair and some get a push one. I understand the people that are not all there not having one, but I have met other people that are all there that have push wheelchairs that are controlled by someone else.

I tried to get one of the stylists to buy the property, as I thought It would be better and initially she said yes. But, after some further deliberation she said she couldn't raise the capital.

I wrote a note for the carers, in the hope it would help them understand me and my condition more.

To all Carers

Please Note

I had 2 strokes, on the 7 March 2004 at about 8am. I blacked out. I was taken to Derriford via Torbay, where I was in intensive care. It was touch and go whether I would make it. I was born 18 July 1961, which makes me nearly 44 when I wrote this. I have 2 sons, Jacob 9, who lives in Abbotskerswell, near Newton Abbot and Jonah 4, who lives with his mum, my girlfriend, in Rome, Italy. I met Claudia in the foothills of the Sierra Nevada, Spain. Claudia was then 27, I was 40. I get to see them about every 5 weeks.

Before my strokes I was quite active, windsurfing, running, going to the gym most nights. Claudia lived here for 2 years, when Jonah (Giona) was born, but didn't like it. When they're not here, I really miss them. I have been to Rome about 30 times, I was going to live there. I had driven over with some boxes and was due to make maybe 2 more trips before I moved over permanently.

I was a hairdresser, owning my own salon in Bovey Tracey. I had 5 girls working for me. I lived above the salon. I have sold it now.

I have one older brother in the RAF in Cyprus, who is about to retire and move to Canada, his wife is Canadian. One older sister that lives near Bovey Tracey.

My mother has been diagnosed with cancer, she has had it before and now chooses not to undergo any treatment. She has a longstanding boyfriend.

My father lives in East Sussex and hasn't been to see me since this happened. We have not really spoken for years.

73

The Best That I Can Be

I am emotionally labile (pronounced lay-bile). It means I am not in control of my emotions. When I laugh, I find it difficult to stop and when I cry—I really cry. Please ignore me if I laugh.

I get frustrated too, if I am not understood.

I am an avid Formula 1 fan and will forgo my meals when it is on.

I like movies.

Drinking is a task for me, so I am very nervous when I drink.

Did you know, I run a higher risk of having another stroke, because I have had one, so I am very paranoid if I get a headache or something.

I am very weak in the mornings, so don't expect me to say anything or do much.

I like routine.

I get very upset if I get wet or dirty. I feel ashamed.

Let me finish on the communication aid, don't jump to any conclusions, although tempting. I don't mind if you finish words for me.

Since my strokes my scalp has become very, very sensitive. I can shake violently, when it is touched or brushed. When my hair is washed, it's terrible. It doesn't hurt. Sometimes I shake violently, if it itches.

I like my own company, but am happy to eat with others.

I like my own independence.

Strokes make me yawn more. So don't comment that I am tired.

My brain seems to function normally, as does my hearing, which is excellent, so there is no need to raise your voice or talk simply. It makes it crueller really that my brain function seems normal.

74

I still ask myself the same question, "Why me?"

I am very bitter about what happened, there's not a day that goes by that I'm not bitter, so I am very serious.

I am writing a book, about my stroke experience. I will probably finish it, around January 2006. To date I have written about 30,000 words. My writing is very slow. I started it about 1 year ago.

Please ensure other carers read this.

CHAPTER FOURTEEN

I started to get depressed, I had stopped the antidepressants some weeks before, thinking I could cope. I was depressed for some time. I started having bad thoughts about what Claudia was doing and I would phone her and I would send her the most horrible texts. One night I rang my bell and asked for my mobile phone, I think it was just gone one – that's just gone two in Italy. I rang Claudia on her mobile. She was not impressed with me phoning at that time, as she was in bed and at her parents. She just couldn't cope with my depressive state. I was so miserable. I was having terrible dreams about her. I was totally paranoid, I was even paranoid about being paranoid. I suppose it's just one of the side effects of having a stroke. It is difficult though, when your girlfriend is so far away and you are so bloody useless.

One morning I asked to see the Manager. I had prepared a speech on my communication aid the night before. I told her I was so low and what I was thinking about Claudia. I cried and cried. She told me not to be silly and that antidepressants were a good thing in certain circumstances and I should consider them again. I was being silly, but I just couldn't help it. About a week later I started a new course of antidepressants, this time I asked for them to be stronger.

I had speech therapy once a week and he, the speech therapist, was trying to get me my own communication aid. It was possible to have an Italian component added to it that was going to be around £500, which I had agreed to finance.

It was agreed that my room would be painted. I chose the colours, a terracotta and an almondy colour. I was quite excited. I was initially told they would paint it in about two weeks, but it took a lot longer, which in hindsight was good.

I don't know why, but my right leg started spasming. It would bend up in bed, resulting in me pressing the call bell and getting a carer to push it down. Sometimes this would happen six or seven times through the night, so I didn't get much sleep. It eventually went down to about once or twice a night, mainly in the mornings, when I first awoke at about half past six.

I was very weak in the mornings, it surprised me how weak I was. Some mornings I couldn't operate my chair initially. I could five minutes later, but it took what strength I had to operate the chair and propel myself forward so I could get to the dining room. I was so weak some mornings that I couldn't tip my cup up to my lips, so I would leave the last bit. Sometimes my weakness stayed with me all day, but mostly it took me until after breakfast, which I guess was about one hour, before I had all my strength – and that wasn't much.

I had slip mats placed under my feet in the wheelchair, the idea being that they would prevent my feet from slipping. They didn't. They helped, but my feet still kept coming off. That was the reason I went into walls, to push my feet back on. They were used on the Standaid, first thing in the morning, but under my feet for the rest of the day. It must have looked odd, me going into walls, especially when I went shopping.

I asked a friend to get me two cases of an energy drink, one case for the carers and one case for the office staff – wasn't that nice of me? Well, if the truth be known, I had been a bit of a pain, choking at mealtimes and screaming. I used to scream if things didn't go right for me and choking and/or coughing usually resulted in me getting wet and I would scream. My legs also went into spasm when I did this. Straight as anything they were. No one could bend them to get them back on the footplates. They were like rods of iron. The carers had to wait until I had calmed down a bit.

My drinks, three of them, were placed on the extension table in front of me, in a row, one behind the other, on the left side of the table. If I didn't choke or cough on them, which I sometimes did (the more watery the drink, the more I seemed to cough) then my knees would bang on the table if my food didn't agree with me, knocking my drinks and slopping out on the table and me. At night, I always had two milky drinks, which caused me one or two problems.

I was very nervous about drinking at the best of times, in case I coughed, or dropped it. My drinking was very slow and deliberate.

When I coughed, I just couldn't put my drink down, so it slopped all over me, or I snorted into my drink, causing it to spray everywhere. My food was cut up small, as I couldn't chew. Occasionally it wasn't cut up small enough and the food would get stuck in my throat and I would choke. I found it very difficult to manoeuvre my food to the back of my mouth, so that I could swallow it. I had to rely on gravity. I couldn't tilt my head back though, as that might prove to be too quick and cause me to choke.

We always had sandwiches on a Sunday. You know, run of the mill stuff like cheese, ham, beef, corned beef, chicken and tuna. We were asked what we wanted by a carer that was there. The old chap that fell asleep a lot also mumbled and when asked what sandwiches he wanted, the carer couldn't quite hear, so she stooped down beside him, so she could hear better, again he muttered one word, which made me laugh so, so much I nearly died. "Crab"! Well, the carer who took his order just couldn't believe it. She repeated his order to the whole dining room, over and over again.

My lability was a big problem: it caused me to laugh so much. When others around me laughed, I laughed even more. This caused me to leave my food and drinks a few times, as it was impossible to eat or drink when I was labile.

One morning I overheard a conversation that was going on outside my door, which I had asked to be left open, between a resident and the Manager. The resident was going out and would get the Manager an energy drink. I rushed after her, the Manager, and got her to follow me back to my room. She then scrabbled under my bed, at my request, and bought out the two cases of energy drink I had bought. I explained with my communication aid that one was for her, the other for the carers, which she was pleasantly surprised about and politely told me I was no trouble.

I was asked if I wanted to join a Stroke Group, with one other resident that I liked. I said yes. The Stroke Group was some miles away, so we were ferried there each week by the home's minibus and brought back by the Stroke Group's minibus, which made me jump each time the doors were slammed shut. I guess there were just over twenty in the group, of different ages, but mainly older. I suppose I was the most severely disabled, with most of them being able to walk and talk. There were others in wheelchairs. It was for two hours. The first hour was normally a discussion about something, then refreshments and biscuits. I didn't partake of anything to eat or drink, as it took me some time to drink and I might choke or make a mess if I ate. How embarrassing. Anyway, I was only used to a cup with no handles, they had proper tea cups. In the second half, we played table games. The one I liked was a numbers game with counters that were numbered. I got so good at that game, I won regularly. They regularly went out, but, as this involved lunch, I always declined, for the same reasons as not having any refreshments.

All nurses and carers are guilty of this... Why do they tell you two minutes, when they mean in the next hour? Surely they have a rough idea of how long they will be. Don't they know that time is a valuable commodity to someone in my position? I am not asking them to drop everything and deal with me. I am a human and I demand that I am treated like one. You wouldn't keep a friend waiting for an hour without calling them, or coming up with a reasonable excuse as to why you are late. Why am I different? I could watch the television or something, but to be kept waiting for up to an hour, or sometimes even longer, just isn't on.

I am doing my best not to make this sound like a diary, but an actual story of courage, hope, stubbornness, determination or just life through my eyes – take your pick. I write what I feel. What I feel, is what you get.

I asked If I could have a phone line installed, so I could get broadband. Of course I could, was the reaction I got.

The stylist that was originally going to buy the property and then said 'no' came back to me. She had recalculated her figures and decided she could just buy it. I said I would always be there for her, no matter what the problem was. We ironed out some details and the wheels of buying and selling were put into action. I had always wanted to sell the property and business to someone I knew.

Claudia came over. It was Friday. This time on her own. When she came over, her parents that lived in Rome always looked after Giona. Leaving him was a bit of an upheaval for her.

Because she thought I would get cold when out, Claudia bought me the brightest, multi-coloured scarf and hat you can imagine. God knows where she bought it, you could see me coming a mile off. I looked like a mobile rainbow. Thank God it wasn't a very cold winter. The carers ridiculed me about that scarf and hat for flipping ages.

We went to a local, cheap supermarket that we always went to before I had the strokes. Alright, we didn't always go to it together. It was my choice. Claudia liked the more expensive ones. Women!

Claudia humoured me and we went in, laughing. I had a sweet tooth for biscuits, so she bought some.

Claudia got me to text some friends and ask them if they would like to go to the cinema. They said yes.

We got a taxi, there and back. The film we watched was a thriller which was mainly shot in Rome. We didn't know that and we kept glancing and smiling at each other each time an area that we both knew came on the screen. When we got back, Claudia went off for a Chinese takeaway. On her return we all (there was one other) scoffed it down, with me making little mess.

It was while we had this meal that Claudia got a phone call on her mobile that her granny had died. I think because there was someone else there, she kept her composure. Well, almost, she did cry a little. I wanted to console her, properly. It was all I could do to reach out to her with my good arm. My left. I wanted to take her in my arms and tell her everything would be alright, but I couldn't. I knew what she meant to her. She was very close, Claudia also lived in her flat. Her granny lived in a nursing home, although she had lived with Claudia's parents for a while, but was moved to a nursing home. The funeral was to be on the Tuesday, but Claudia was due to be with me till the Wednesday.

The visitor left and Claudia and I went to my room. She cried some more, in between which we discussed the possibility of her going back to Rome for the funeral. It would mean her leaving the next day, which was a Monday. I lied through my teeth, saying it would be okay.

I didn't sleep much that night. I loved her being next to me, but deep down I understood that she should go and be next to her mother.

The next morning Claudia came early. I knew what it meant. I cried even when I saw her at the window, but when she came in I was totally inconsolable. I was still in bed and the bed shook with the ferocity of my crying. She only stayed for half an hour and when she left I was left feeling empty. A great sense of loss came over me. I was devastated. I am sure that leaving me was difficult for her. I stayed in bed all day, refusing any food or drink that was offered to me. I just lay there thinking about Claudia and what we had done in the few days we had shared together.

Because I didn't drink, I got one mother of a headache the following morning. I asked for two paracetamol, which I got, along with the Manager, who explained to me that I was dehydrated and suggested that I should eat and drink that day. It was a new day, so I agreed.

CHAPTER FIFTEEN

I settled back into my life. The stronger antidepressants were fully in my system now. I regularly ordered fresh lilies for my horticultural room, which were delivered now and I was back on my diet.

The phone engineers came to install my phone line. I was quite amused, because they took about six goes to bring the cable in from outside. Eventually, after going in and out, the engineer managed to get it through. They just couldn't get it through the wall to meet up with the internal cable at the junction box. I got the broadband connection about a week later, through a friend. He installed everything · on the laptop for me later.

I bought an answer phone with a hands free facility, so that I could speak to Claudia. I was so pleased that she could understand ninety percent of what I said on the phone. I kept my words simple and if she didn't understand me, I tried to say it in another way.

I went on the internet now most nights and I found it quite informative. I got some information for a bonsai tree I had ordered from the local flower shop and my mother found out what it was called. She also bought me some literature on bonsais.

I laughed so much one night, as one of the carers that put me to bed was wearing bright pink, fluffy slippers because they were comfortable. She then ridiculed me about my scarf and hat. I was able to ridicule her about her slippers, which she understood. She did look ridiculous though, in her pale blue uniform and bright pink fluffy slippers.

My key worker changed again to a new chap who had bad body odour (lucky me!). A senior nurse told me my old one had left. You can imagine my surprise when he was working a week later. About a week later, he did leave.

There I was eating my dinner one day and my brother just popped up. The last time I saw him was at Torbay hospital. He was going to be here for five days.

We went to a local pub with my brother-in-law also. It was the first time in a pub for me, since my new life, so I was very wary. I told my brother about my lability – he thought it was a spelling mistake on my communication aid. I explained what it was and how it affected me. What do you do in pubs? Drink. What do I find hard to do? Drink. I ordered a drink and a packet of crisps, knowing that the drink might be a problem. To my surprise, I managed nearly all of it and soon ordered another orange juice. As for the crisps, it was my first time, but I knew I could manage them and I did.

My two comical friends, who came to the cinema before, had been threatening to take me to the cinema again and one of them just texted me out of the blue asking if I wanted to go to the cinema. I asked my brother who agreed. So next day we went to the cinema again. We saw a film full of demons and it made me jump a few times. It even made them jump, so you can imagine how much I jumped. Because of my success with crisps before, I had crisps while I watched the film. They were in a big box, of which I managed most of them. My brother tried to order a taxi to go back, but there were no wheelchair taxis available, so we walked. It took about forty-five minutes and we stopped for some chips along the way, which was nice.

Whenever I went out, I had a pad on, which can best be described as a nappy for adults. It was put on in the Standaid and kept me from having accidents. I have to say most of the time when I briefly went out I didn't use the pad, but it did offer me security, if I needed it for longer periods.

It was while my brother was here, and I was giving him a guided tour of the building, that we went into an empty room for me to turn round. It was massive and empty. You could fit my room in there twice over and still have some space left. It was initially someone else's, but they had unfortunately died. I rushed off to see the Manager. You know what I am thinking, don't you?

I asked her if I should move. She didn't give me an immediate answer, because the room was so far from the carer's office and from what she knew I needed a lot of attention.

It was one of the last rooms in the building and to get to it meant going down a long corridor, then turning sharp left, then sharp right. Because the corridors were so narrow, I had to manoeuvre myself very slowly around the corners and eventually into the room.

She was concerned about my legs spasming all night, which they had been, but I told her it was only in the mornings now. She said that the bike should help my legs when it came and to give it till the end of the week, concerning the room. I gave it two weeks.

On Jerry's advice, I downloaded a music programme, it gave me hours of amusement. I was able to get all my favourite pieces of music and where I could, I got the videos as well. I even got some cartoons for Giona, even though he didn't understand them, as they were in English. I did manage to get some Italian music though.

Claudia was due to come over, just after my brother went back.

My brother went to chase up my cushion, my control, so that it hinged back and my speed (to make it faster) on my wheelchair. He bought me a nice oil lamp before he went back, which was switched on each night.

He also asked the Manager about the big room and was told I was pencilled in.

I tried my hardest to control my bladder and I didn't scream if it was urgent, hoping that it would filter back to the Manager that I was less demanding.

I was visited, at last, by the hospital physiotherapist. It only took from early January till late March. She asked me lots of questions, then assessed me in the prone position. After her assessment, she told me that I wouldn't be getting any extra physiotherapy. That was going to be her recommendation. She did organise a new hand splint though, mine was getting rather grubby and the position made it hard to put on, and she ordered a small T-roll. She also told me something I didn't want to hear: "You will never walk again". To come out with a statement like that was very unprofessional, I thought. Why not say "You MAY never walk again"? See the difference: one gives hope, as there is always hope. The other is so final. Before I knew I had wonky hips, I even asked her why one leg was about two inches shorter. She said it was because I wasn't sitting straight and if I did, it would eliminate the problem. Now, you would have thought she would know, being a qualified physiotherapist, but she didn't. She even ordered me a new arm splint and when it came, she gave me verbal instructions for how to put it on. It should have been put on the other way, as it was only hinged one way. The way that she recommended meant the elbow couldn't bend into the body only out, so if you break my elbow joint, you can bend it. Silly woman, why didn't she read the instructions that came with it? I didn't like her, she had a very nonchalant attitude, no doubt she fitted in well to the National Health Service directive.

I wasn't happy because Torbay promised a care package and after sending an e-mail to my social worker, she decided it would be best if all three of us met up to talk about it. When we met, the social worker said her hands were tied and the physiotherapist stuck to her guns about her assessment. When I said I would get private physiotherapy, she went along with it, saying it was a good idea. Isn't that called a contradiction? My independence was discussed and it was agreed to escort me down to the seafront and then, after doing it a few times and if I was safe, I could go on my own.

A lady came to visit me from the Stroke Association. It was the nearest thing to a psychotherapist that the doctor could come up with. A lady from the Stroke Association definitely wasn't the same as a trained psychotherapist, or was I being picky? She soon stopped coming.

My social worker, so she said, was in the process of contacting a psychotherapist. All in all, it took her one year and that's only because my new speech therapist intervened later.

I was dirty one night and the carer cleaned me up with hard surface wipes. I complained they stung. The other carers pointed out that the wipes should just be used on surfaces, as they contained bleach. They never came back and apologised to me for causing me discomfort.

Eventually, through badgering and recommendation, I was offered more physiotherapy, three weeks worth (woopedoo!) and further physiotherapy if I improved. What was the likelihood of me improving over three weeks? Over three months they might see a minor improvement, but not three weeks. As sure as eggs are eggs I wasn't offered any more.

By use of a webcam, I was able to not only chat with my brother in Cyprus, but see him as well.

When Claudia came over with Giona for Easter 2005, she had brought the biggest chocolate Easter egg you have ever seen – it was for me – with a slightly smaller one for Jacob. Claudia's parents had given her a packet of individually wrapped chocolate eggs, which her and Giona unwrapped for me and placed them back in the bag, most of which I gave out as presents, to the staff or anyone that came in my room really.

Although I sat waiting by my window for them to arrive and then went out to the door to meet them, I noticed that I wasn't emotional this time. I did wonder if Claudia noticed.

While she and Giona were here, we went to the cinema, this time with my sister and her children. I had some crisps which Claudia was a bit wary about, until I reassured her that I would be okay.

One night we went out for a meal, the four of us, to the pizza restaurant we went to before and I said yes to a drink, which I managed. The children had a blue gas balloon each, which was meticulously carried into the taxi, only for Claudia to let go of Giona's balloon when we got back to Oldway, when she got Giona out of the taxi. Up, up and away it went, until it completely vanished in the early evening sky. No matter what we did, Giona was totally inconsolable. It was as if his life depended on it.

We mostly ate in the room this time, so that Giona and/or Jacob could watch the television while they ate.

We walked into the town, hoping to get a taxi back, but there was none available, so we walked back. I wanted to take the children to a toy shop, as it was Easter, and buy them a present each, which we did. Giona soon chose his, but Jacob just took ages.

I showed Claudia the room I was hoping to move into.

We went down to the beach and the children were very keen to play on the sand. Jacob soon elbowed his way into a football game, which he had been watching and helping from the side lines. Giona was just content to play in the sand.

It was a relaxed and enjoyable time that was due to come to an abrupt end, again.

My dream of fatherhood soon finished when Claudia and Giona went back. I cried, even though the children were there. It was all too much for me. I cried. I knew I wouldn't see her for a few weeks.

Before she left, Claudia broke up that egg she had bought for me, put it in a cardboard tray and put it in a drawer. It was very thick and dark, not milk like we get over here, but plain and very sweet on the palate.

She also brought me some soft Italian chocolates and as they were wrapped in foil, I was able to open them. As I was on a diet, I seldom ate them, choosing instead, to give them as thank you's to carers and cleaners. I had the egg, but most everything else I gave away. I was sad, but settled into my life without Claudia, without my family. It was just something I had to learn to except, or adapt to. I told you, it was cruel.

While Claudia was over, she did ask many times if I could go to a swimming pool again, as this seemed to accelerate my improvement. She was told each time that it would be looked into, but nothing ever came of it. I had a visit to the hospital to visit the OTs' department for a new hand splint, as the straps on mine were getting a bit tatty and the carers were having difficulty getting the wrist to sit in properly. I saw a nice OT, who made me a new one.

They took your blood pressure and pulse each week and sometimes if I got ill or had a headache, I would get totally paranoid and ask for my blood pressure to be taken. I got less paranoid as the months went on.

I was a little nervous the day I asked the Manager about the room, because I didn't know what her reaction would be. The new room was much bigger than my room and it would be better for me. You could wheel the Standaid in and manoeuvre it around better and the exercise bike I was due to get would fit in better. But, she was concerned about the level of care I needed. She said she would speak to the care assistants first. It was a Friday, so I had one more weekend in my room before the decision would be made.

It was a lunchtime, I was in the dining room and the Manager walked in. I managed to catch her eye, she came over to me, she knew what I wanted to ask her, but the word "Room" was too much for me to say, it was such a big thing. She smiled down at me and told me I could move into the room on the Friday.

CHAPTER SIXTEEN

T hat week was a busy week. My T-bar arrived, much smaller than the one I used at Rowans. I had straps fitted to my wheelchair to prevent my feet flying off and it stopped them banging on my dinner table. It was the first week of my private physiotherapist, my first week of going out to be assessed, my masseur came... Yes, for me it was a busy week.

I also went to the doctors, not that there was anything wrong, but to ask about something I had read on the internet. I was already on quite a high dose of baclofen (that's the muscle relaxant), but I had read that you could get it fed directly to your spine, via an implanted pump, which was very successful. Intrathecal was the correct terminology and the pump stored the baclofen and fed very small amounts into the spine. The pump is placed under the skin and you have to have a fresh supply of baclofen every once in a while, which is injected in. I found out about it, quite by accident, on the internet. I was told a specialist would contact me.

There was one resident, who came in on respite care for two weeks. Thank God it was only two weeks. He lived many, many miles away, but chose Oldway as his holiday home. He came about twice a year. He constantly followed the carers about. He breathed very heavily—this was an indicator to him being close in the vicinity and I am sure the carers used to run in the other direction when they heard him coming. They constantly sent him on errands for them, just so they could have a rest from him no doubt. He would run everywhere in the home, he was like a horse, snorting and galloping all over the place. He had his own mobility scooter, to go outside. It's like he was on a diet of long life batteries. He couldn't speak and called everybody the same name, either ooogh, or aaagh and he sounded like Chewbacca, the hairy wookie from Star Wars. He had a communication aid which he seldom used, instead he wrote out the abbreviated words, letter by letter, with his finger, on walls and doors or any surface available. He always wanted you to converse with him, which was a laborious task anyway, to the point of being annoying and getting away from his "Conversations" was an art form in itself. He was banned from the staff room and the kitchen, but he still went in there, so there was no getting away from him. He was about my age, a bit older and of course not so handsome (shame he didn't act it). He always went to bed late, sometimes four or five o'clock and he loved his football. Did he get tired with his late night goings on? Unfortunately not. He came into my room one evening, because I had visitors who encouraged him. One of them liked football, but the uninvited guest knew more and mimed his way through football trivia for about an hour. The carers didn't mind, even though they could see I was in a dilemma, they were just glad he was out of their hair for a while. He came into my room again on another night and he told me one of the carers was silly. I corrected him by saying one of the carers was a bitch. This he found amusing and galloped off to show the carers what was written on the communication aid. He asked me to write some more, which I did. He liked me. When he left, he wrote letters, which I got a mention in and rung the carers. God knows what he said, or if he said anything intelligible. He was due to come back in about five months, God help us.

My key worker changed to a young girl that I got on with and she didn't have body odour, but she was very forgetful.

I couldn't go into the room until the Friday, as there was someone in there on respite care who was not due to leave until the Thursday. On Thursday night I went down there. I weighed up how the bed should be, the wardrobes, there were two and the two chests of drawers.

They were all in pine and although they all didn't exactly match, they looked good, along with a big table, where I could put my laptop. Oh, and two big comfy chairs. The toilet and sink were en suite and it had five windows that faced west, with five smaller windows at the top. The red, yellow and green flowers on the two lampshades matched the windows.

It was split in two parts. Where the bed was going and where the wardrobes were was the biggest.

Twelve foot by fourteen foot, I guess: that's where the en suite was – and an extension area that was about twelve foot by seven foot: that's where the windows, comfy chairs and table were. So, overall it was about twelve foot by twenty-one foot. As it faced directly onto the road, it had net curtains, so people could not see in. Yes, I lost my view, but I had gained a much bigger room.

Two carers helped me move in and arrange things as I wanted them and I bought them and the Manager a plant each, just to say thank you. I had lots more space, it was the biggest room in the house. It had a narrow shelf, on the picture rail, which ran round most of the room. I bought some small model cars to place on that, along with some of my trinkets and, as my room was now bigger, I bought some more plants to fill it.

I had so many plants now, just over twenty-five, and that didn't include the four exotic plants on the window sill that didn't need water, as they were in a funny gel that fed them. I suppose they lasted about three months and then my mum replaced them with new ones. Then there were the flowers, they were mostly lilies, but sometimes they were replaced by carnations, or any other cut flowers my mum could get hold of, but mostly it was lilies that graced the centre of my window sill. She came and watered all my plants each week, apart from my two bonsai, carers would water them each morning or as I wanted.

The table wasn't quite high enough, but that was soon rectified with a wooden strip, which still wasn't quite high enough and then temporarily raised by some video cases and later by some wooden blocks. I now had access to my laptop twenty-four hours a day.

I found that I got more spasms, particularly when writing. Why, I don't know, perhaps it was something to do with concentration. I didn't get it when I surfed the net, just when I wrote this story.

One day I needed a wee and I closed my door, managed to get everything off my lap and on to the bed, get the bottle, undo my zip and popper, get myself out, place the bottle, which was just reachable in the bathroom and have a wee, put the bottle back on the bed and zip myself up, the popper was too difficult for me. I was so pleased. I rang for a carer to empty my bottle and finish doing me up and told them, I was so happy, I could hardly spell out what I had done. The carer hugged me, I think she was as excited as me. It was a great achievement. That had been a goal of mine that I thought was a long time away. So now I can wee on my own, I still call for someone to empty it. I zip myself back up, I don't undo the popper or top button and put the things back on my lap. Some trousers are more difficult than others, but most are okay. I still get wet on occasions, when my body catches me out, but most of the time I manage.

Before Claudia came over, for a flying visit, only three days this time, I asked her to get me two bright T-shirts and some shorts. Everything was bright. One of the T-shirts was bright pink, which I liked, which the laundry staff forgot to wash separately. Everything went pink and had to be bleached, so I was told. I was waiting for Claudia outside. I was so happy to see her, I cried.

She liked my new room, she had only seen it empty. Claudia and I went to a toy shop, not only to buy something for Giona, who had stayed in Rome, with his grandparents, but to buy some big model cars for me, which were placed on my window sill, between the plants and flowers that I had.

Afterwards we went to our pizza restaurant again, where I managed to flick the fork over the other side of the room, because one of the staff dropped a pan on the floor and it scared me and made me jump. We laughed so much. I knew that my time with her was limited and it soon came to her going, which made me cry.

I got on with things and my bike soon arrived to go in my new room, which I was very keen to go on. At Rowans it was set for fifteen minutes, but I set mine for twenty. I did arms first. I could grip with my left, but my right had to be strapped on with a purpose-made

Velcro strap. My feet were also placed on the foot pedals, they too were strapped into place with Velcro straps.

Then I was ready. I had my phone and the bell, which at first was placed under my right leg, so it didn't slip. Later it was placed where the armrests had come from, they had to be removed, or the arm pedals of the bike caught it. Removing them was quite simple, just a finger screw held them on.

Then in the beginning I was also given my television remote. Later I had a CD on. I did about one hour in total, arms and legs most every night, although not together, it didn't work like that, but independently.

I had a total of four escorted trips out, then I was assessed on my ability to go out on my own. They were confident with me. I stopped at all the right places and used crossings where I could. I could now go out on my own. So long as it was locally.

I regularly went to a DVD shop to hire out a film. I loved films, especially long ones, the longer the better. Why, well long films just had to be good, didn't they? Fridays was like an assault course, as Friday was bin day. Bins would be strewn across the pavement, making my passage difficult. Many was the time that I had to divert on to the road.

I had been practising a new signature as I was originally right handed and the bank had okayed it, even though it looked different on occasions. I tried to keep still, when I was signing, but sometimes I would sniff, then there would be a line all the way off the cheque or paper I was signing. Seeing this would make me laugh, then there was no way in hell I was capable of signing anything.

I was still on my diet. Why is it easier to put on weight than to lose it? I think I will stay on a permanent diet.

I was very keen on watching Formula 1, both the qualifying and the race. No one, except Claudia, if she was over, could stop me watching it. If it coincided with mealtimes, I missed my meal and a couple of times it was on, live, very early in the morning and guess who woke up to watch it? I set my alarm on my mobile phone that was always on my lap, but I didn't really need that, as I was already awake.

I decided on a fish tank for my room and when I mentioned it to the Manager, she said I could have theirs. The fish tank they had had tropical fish in it. I wanted coldwater fish, as they were easier to look after. Before my strokes, I had owned two coldwater fish, so I knew they were easier to look after. I was told I could have it soon. But soon turned out to be a very long time. I knew of a quite local aquarium centre and I asked the Manager if I could take myself along there. As she was much more confident in my abilities, she agreed and one afternoon I went along there and chose four fish, the rest were to be chosen by Claudia and the children. I told them I was promised the home's fish tank, which was quite new, I hasten to add.

Generally, it was much quieter in my new room. I say generally, because of two reasons.

Firstly I was next to the smoking room, which was where the staff went most of the time on their breaks, as they were not allowed to smoke in the staff room/nurses' station and I could hear their voices coming through the wall, as part of the wall was plaster board. Eventually the owner asked them not to smoke in there, as it was a residents' smoking lounge and they were using it like a staff room. It was better for me, when they were banned, as most of the residents didn't smoke and the few that did smoked in their room most of the time, which meant I didn't get so much secondary smoke in my room. Secondly, I now lived opposite a tall, schizophrenic monk, who shouted a lot at an imaginary friend. As I generally kept my door open, you could hear him ranting and raving behind his closed door. When he was very mad, as he didn't have a toilet in his room, you would quite often hear him come out his room, slam the door, walk into the bathroom next door to him, flush the toilet and walk back into his room muttering. I heard him shout "How do you like that then?" to his imaginary friend, although I don't know what satisfaction it gave him, to abruptly flush the toilet? (Honestly, I think I was living in a nut house). If he wasn't ranting and raving, he would just, spontaneously, burst into laughter. He knew about his behaviour and would quite often apologise for his outbursts. He was kind though.

He would quite often walk past my room and give me a cheery "Hello". He even popped in sometimes, to give me some fudge and if I had visitors he would make a point of asking them if they wanted a drink.

At last I was given my own communication aid. It was very, very similar to my old one, which was sent back to Torbay Hospital, where it was on loan from. Mine didn't have the choice of voices the old one had: the old one had about six, while mine just had male and female choices.

Mine did have the Italian component – not that I could speak Italian fluently, but I could now say simple things to Giona, which was important for me.

Just after that, my speech therapist changed to a "youngish" girl. She was very good, I really liked her: she had a very strong, professional attitude.

I would never give myself credit for achieving things. I was happy inside for doing it, but I was convinced I could do better. I was criticised heavily for this, by carers and professionals alike, but I am sure that my stubbornness and my non-acceptance keeps me going forward. I am not one to accept things, my situation will improve, I don't know how long it will take, or how much, but it will improve, I will make it by achieving more and more.

I became so tidy conscious: everything in my room, had to be in a certain place and a certain way and I hated clutter. I liked things to be balanced, like my flowers (oh, I wish my partner was like that, you mutter under your breath).

I discovered that I was allergic to meat substitute. It affected my bowels. When I voluntarily stopped having it (which I did on occasions) my bowels were okay. It took me many months to discover this and lots of surfing the net and reading lots of articles. It was annoying really, as no one really believed me, but some people do get upset stomachs from it. I was okay before my strokes, but I guess I was a little more fragile now.

Whenever I went out or every afternoon before tea (weather permitting, of course) I would wear a bandana. Later, I wore them all day, as my hair was getting longer. I had a full head of thick hair and it hadn't started receding. I wore bandanas before my strokes, so I had quite a collection already, which I added to. I think I have about twenty. I wore them more to keep my hair tidy than as a fashion statement. My hair was nearly down to my shoulders, as I wanted to grow it, so I could just tie it back. As I went out most days, if the weather was nice, a bandana kept the wind from blowing the hair in my face – well, that was my excuse.

CHAPTER SEVENTEEN

I had a bright red futon in my old flat, so I asked if Claudia and the boys could stay on occasions, I was told they could. I sent a text to some friends, asking if they could bring it over. It easily slotted into where the two chairs were. So it was in place for when they came over. I went out and bought a double quilt and a cover for it.

I sold both the flat and the business, at last. There were lots of hurdles to get over. My money went in my business account, until it was eventually closed. Most of it was swallowed up by the dreaded VAT/tax man and the accountant.

When Claudia and Giona came over, one of the places we visited was Dartmoor. Claudia phoned the Dartmoor head office to find out where I could go. It was a long taxi ride. Claudia, Giona and Jacob came in the taxi with me. My sister, her husband, her three children and my mum met us there. Because it was difficult to find and the taxi driver had to negotiate very narrow roads and it took about an hour to get there, the taxi driver decided he would stay there. We walked along a tarmac lane that was only used by service vehicles. The children kept going down to the bubbling stream that ran parallel to the winding, single track road which I trundled along. It rained, not heavy, more a heavy mist really, but that didn't dampen our spirits. The children were happy to paddle in the water.

The day before we also went, with my mum, on the local steam railway that ran to Dartmouth, which incidentally I could hear drifting into my room. Both children were very excited. I could only go in the goods van, which was okay, as someone had thoughtfully put some seats in there. We caught the ferry across the river Dart and had about an hour in Dartmouth where we got an ice cream. Mine was in a cup and Claudia had to feed me and then it was time to go back.

We visited the local aquarium centre, where both the children and Claudia chose a fish to go in my aquarium. I had chosen four fish on a previous visit, on my own, if you remember. Because Oldway were taking so long over the fish tank, I had decided to order a new one, which I ordered the same day, along with a purpose-made cabinet for it to stand on. I ordered a slightly bigger tank than the one I had been previously promised.

Jacob had a foldaway scooter that I had bought him some years before. It was kept in the car and whenever we planned to go down the road to the seafront, we took it. When we got there, Jacob would hold onto the back of the wheelchair and standing on his scooter, I was able to pull him along. Giona was too small for this, although he did sit on my lap on occasions, with him using the horn, like a train whistle.

Poor Giona didn't understand why I was crying when it was time for them to go. I wasn't going to see them until August, now it was June, they would miss my birthday on the eighteenth of July and I would miss Giona's on the twenty-ninth. All of July without seeing them! It was going to be difficult.

Claudia didn't stay every night, more like every other night. She also stayed with a close friend of hers, about one hour away. She was married and had two young children, one of them being about Giona's age.

One of the cleaners, who later became an activities co-ordinator, of which there are two, got hold of an electric, mobility scooter. I thought it was very cheap. I couldn't use it, but lots of the residents could, so I bought it for the residents. They already had one, a red one, this one was blue. They accepted it and were very grateful to me. I bought it because it was cheap and the home did a lot for me.

One thing I never understood: there was a couple of people, at least, who seemed like they didn't belong there. I am sure they were quite capable of looking after themselves, so why were they there?

For a few weeks I had a bad big toe on my right foot. The cause wasn't really explained to me, although it was probably an in-growing toenail that Claudia had cut, about two months before. Unlike my finger nails, my toe nails grew very slowly. My toe swelled up. It was pink and very painful.

An appointment was made for me to see the local G.P. who put me on a week's worth of antibiotics. They were just great – they gave me diarrhoea and I had to wear a pad every day, as my bowels were likely to open spontaneously, and they did. What with all the wiping, I was very, very sore. They also played havoc with my bladder. In all, I was on three courses of antibiotics, as my toe wasn't responding, each one stronger than the other, so you can imagine how much it affected my bladder and bowels. Eventually the antibiotics worked.

I updated my note:

To all Carers

Please Note

And tell others to read it!

I don't write this stuff for the hell of it, it's to help you!

I had 2 strokes in March 2004. Am I bitter? I should say so. I was very fit and healthy.

I still ask myself the same question: "Why me?"

I am emotionally labile (pronounced lay-bile) it means I am not in control of my emotions. When I laugh, I find it difficult to stop and when I cry, I really cry. Please ignore me if I laugh. Some carers still comment on my smiling and laughing. Guess what? I CAN'T HELP IT, I AM LABILE.

The Best That I Can Be

I get frustrated too, if I am not understood. So, please give me the communication aid (Box), it's my only way of communicating with you.

I am very stubborn, I know my own mind.

Drinking is a task for me, so I am very nervous when I drink, I keep thinking I will spill or drop it.

Sometimes when I eat and drink, I cough. This is not to be confused with choking, where I'm gasping for air, it's just a cough. It's only when I get upset, because I'm wet, you need to worry. Same as sneezing. I do such a big sneeze.

I like routine.

I get very upset, if I get wet or dirty. I feel ashamed.

Let me finish on the communication aid, don't jump to any conclusions, although tempting. I don't mind if you finish words for me, but please don't guess.

Since my strokes my scalp has become very, very sensitive. I can shake violently, when it is touched or brushed. When my hair is washed, it's terrible. It doesn't really hurt. Not washing it causes more irritation, so does gel and some shampoos (so I've discovered) which does hurt, so I might ask for it to be washed on occasion. Sometimes I shake violently, if it itches.

As I'm very jumpy and if the door is closed, please don't knock abruptly and/or barge in. I would prefer you don't knock and put your head around the door and quietly call my name.

I like my own company, but am happy to eat with others.

I like my own independence.

I like all music, really. I used to be a DJ in a club that catered for all tastes, from Big Band right through to the latest Club music.

Strokes make me yawn more. So don't comment that I am tired. I'm not. It winds me up if you comment I'm tired.

My brain seems to function normally, as does my hearing, which is excellent, so there is no need to raise your voice or talk simply. It makes it crueller really that my brain function seems normal.

I am writing a book, about my stroke experience. I hoped to finish it around January 2006. I won't. I don't know when I will finish it now. To date, I have written just over 30,000 words. Maybe, when I get close to 50,000 words, I will be happy. My writing is very slow. I started it in about July 2004.

I may not show it, but I do appreciate what you do for me.

Please ensure other carers read this. When you've finished reading, it might be an idea to put your initials at the bottom that way, you will know who's read it and you won't assume.

The carer had had problems with her car alarm before, it just went off on its own. Still she chose to park it outside my window when she was on nights. One night in particular she had parked it directly outside my window, I was just about to have the first sip of my two milky "bedtime" drinks, when the car alarm went off. I jumped abruptly. The drink I was holding went all over me. I was soaked. I got to the bell, screaming, which was always placed on my bed. The car alarm went off again for no reason. I rang and the carer whose car it was answered and she guessed what it was, when I was just able to point to the car. I stopped having the drinks soon after that, not because of that incident, but because of their calorific content.

There was one carer who every time she spoke, I would interpret in a sexual nature. So she was very careful with her words, but no matter how hard she tried, she managed to say something that would have me in fits of laughter.

"Blimey, it's so stiff this morning" referring to the tightness in my legs. "Is it too tight?" referring to doing up my leg splints. "Is it comfortable?" referring to anything. "I can't get it in" referring to my footplates that were constantly taken off, every time they used the Standaid. "Every time I come in this room, I make him laugh" referring to entering into my room. So you can see, anything she said I misinterpreted it.

One day I was in hysterics, as she said one thing after another which had a sexual connotation. She was with another carer and they had to sit down on the bed, they were laughing so much, as they couldn't keep standing up. Only her though, no one else. I can't put my finger on why I found just her so funny, but I did.

The fish tank had to have some of the water removed about every week. I had an empty flower pot for this task and it was twelve pots out and twelve pots in, plus some chemicals which I measured in drops, two for every pot. At first I asked the carers to do this, until it was pointed out by the Manager that they shouldn't do it and it was up to me to ask one of my visitors to do it. I asked my mum. She came regularly every week and changed my flowers and saw to my plants, whilst her partner saw to my fish tank. I did lose some fish and they were hooked out with a net I had, by whoever was in my room at the time, doing a different job. I would notice one fish was missing and nine times out of ten, I would spy one floating. I was very thoughtful about their burial: they would be flushed down the toilet.

Whenever it was sunny, I went in the garden to sunbathe. My T-shirt was taken off and oil, of my own concoction, was liberally spread on my tummy, chest, face and arms. It had no protection in it, as I found it difficult to catch the sun and go brown. My trousers were left on, as I had medical stockings on. I could stay in the sun for hours, which I did. I didn't go brown really, just a dark honey colour, pale honey in the winter. I had to be careful around my eyes, as I had vitiligo (no melanin) there. I wore protection around there, otherwise it easily burnt, swelled and went bright pink. Even wearing some protection, I still looked like a panda, or as if I had worn sunglasses. Then at the end of my sunbathing session, I would go back in and have the oily concoction wiped off. It would go all over my armrests and control, so they were wiped too.

I found I could suck from a straw, which was great for me, as I could comfortably drink when I went out with Claudia, and at mealtimes I would no longer leave the last bit in the cup, as I couldn't tip the cup up enough. I could get the last eighth with a straw. Sounds great in principle, but I couldn't catch that damn straw on occasions, it just evaded my mouth. Many was the time that I chased it round the cup, especially if they were bent over, as they were bendy straws. Why do people automatically bend them? I would manage to take them out and straighten them again.

At last I was contacted by the hospital specialist about the intrathecal baclofen, offering me an appointment to see him. I went to that appointment, where the specialist explained to me about intrathecal baclofen. He told me that in my case it wasn't for me and that the oral baclofen I was on was adequate. I forgot to ask him if I needed to continue with the medical stockings: I knew there was an oral alternative. So I wrote to him, explaining about my level of activity on the bike. I was up to at least one hour a day, sometimes more. It would be many months before I heard anything.

I was using my stationary bike quite regularly now, most nights in fact. I would do about twenty minutes on my arms, then when I had finished I would attempt to turn the arms on their own, which was difficult at first, but I managed to do it, albeit very, very slowly. Then I would do two twenty minute sessions on my legs. I always found I could do more in my second twenty minute session. My improvement was hardly noticeable, but I did improve, not each time though, perhaps every three months. Whilst I was on my bike, I did my Oromotor exercises, which the speech therapist had given me. I had them sticky tacked to my wall, so they were by my bike:

OROMOTOR EXERCISES

1.   Ooo. Ooo. Ooo. Ooo. Ooo.

2.   Eee. Eee. Eee. Eee. Eee.

3.   Aaah. Aaah. Aaah. Aaah

4.   Ooo eee aah. Ooo. Eee. Aaah. Ooo. Eee. Aaah. Ooo. Eee.
      Aaah. Ooo. Eee. Aaah.

5.   Lips closed, try pushing air in your cheeks

6.   Baa. Baa. Baa. Baa. Baa.

7.   Push tongue out, as far as you can and move it from side to
      side
7b.   „ „ „ „ „ „ „ up and down

8.   Push tongue as hard as you can, into inside of left cheek
8b.   „ „ „ „ , „ „ of right cheek

9.   Laa. Laa. Laa. Laa. Laa.

10.   Screw up your eyes as tightly as possible

11.   Wrinkle your nose

12.   Do a big frown

13.   Do a big smile

14.   Count as many as you can on one breath

15.   Try and do a shhh for as long as you can on one breath

16.   Try and count as many as possible, on one breath, starting off
      quietly and getting louder and louder

Some exercises were harder than others, especially the "Push tongue as hard as you can, into inside of left then right cheek". I could just about do it to the left (that was weak) but could I do it to the right. "Moving the tongue up and down and side to side" I also found difficult, and boy did those exercises make my mouth ache!

I found a shaver web site, by accident again and it recommended that I use a different shaver for my type of growth (which was very tough) and my sensitive skin. A top of the range foil type was recommended and I found another web site where they were much, much cheaper. After reading all the reviews I could find, I ordered one and just hoped it was better than my rotary shaver. It soon arrived and I was eager to use it. I wasn't disappointed. It was much closer than my rotary one, so close, I would say it was as good, or even better, than a wet shave and no razor burn, which I always got with my old one. Just shows how good a top of the range shaver is.

You certainly pay for it, but what a difference! It even came with a special shaver station that not only charged it, but cleaned it as well, so it was like new each time. I was so impressed, I went back to the website from where I bought it and wrote two rave reviews on it.

I don't know what gave me the idea (probably, the extortionate cost of taxis), but I looked for my own car, on the internet. I found a garage that not only specialised in converting vehicles for the wheelchair bound, but had a good stock of used, converted vehicles as well and they were fairly local. I got a taxi to the garage where I said what I was interested in. There were a few cars I had seen on their web site. I settled on the first one, without seeing the rest. It was deep red and apart from the passenger seat, it had two smaller seats at the back, where I could be anchored between the two.

The salesman anchored me down and strapped me in, then took me on a test drive. Even though it was a diesel, I thought it was quite nippy. He took me through some country lanes, then on a dual carriageway and back again. I was very interested. I haggled a little on the price and we settled in the middle, which gave me £300 off. The total price was £9,600. I said I didn't like the wheel trims and could they be changed, with another vehicle there that was the same type. I did the necessary paperwork and the taxi arrived to take me back, just as I was finishing.

I kept it a secret from Claudia, but soon told everyone else. I ordered a key ring, off the internet, shiny chrome and heart shaped. When it arrived, I sought out a local engravers and had the words "Remember it's a diesel" put on it, as some weeks before Claudia had broken down in my old car, which was a diesel, because she had put petrol in it. I had decided that I only wanted Claudia to drive and the insurance and breakdown cover proved quite a task.

When the car was delivered, about one and a half weeks later, the home allowed me to park it and leave it in their car park.

What a surprise it would be for Claudia!

I longed to be independent. That was my goal. It was discussed that I could get my own place. Claudia had said that Italy was completely out of the question, as I would be much better looked after in the United Kingdom, as there were no Social Services in Italy, benefits would be negligible and I would find the language difficult as I only spoke a little Italian. Under a special scheme, if I could pay the most I could, the council would contribute the rest. It would be in my own interest to put down the most I could, as any money I had left over might affect my benefits. I was told it would take a long time (didn't everything?).

In another meeting I was told that regular funding for my children would be impossible. I was very disappointed.

I had also been looking on web sites at better chairs and I discovered one that not only tilted and reclined, it could raise up as well. It could go 8mph, while my current one's maximum speed was 4mph. It could go a lot further too, nearly 30 miles and it had suspension and lights.

The problem was it was very, very expensive, about the price of a small car. Could I justify that? I quickly weighed up all the pro's and con's and whether I could afford one. I read what I could on it and set my heart on it. I ordered one, in blue.

CHAPTER EIGHTEEN

I was waiting outside for Claudia and Giona. I was very excited, not only because they were coming, but because of the car. I had it all worked out. I couldn't prepare anything on the communication aid; what I said, had to be spontaneous, or she might guess. They arrived. I didn't cry any more. I had stopped some months before. After we did our initial greeting, we purposely walked past the new car and I typed in "That's what we want, something like that". Claudia responded "But they're very expensive, whose is it?" "Someone's in the home" I didn't lie, did I? I produced and gave Claudia a box, containing the key on the key ring. I had been keeping the box under my fleece. She opened it and was gobsmacked.

The car was registered in my name, but Claudia was the driver. It was very comfortable and, so I am told, very easy to drive. It was great being in the back, between the boys, although when they both started singing, or making silly noises, I wished I wasn't there. Claudia soon got the knack of anchoring me down and strapping me in. Some might say it's a waste of a car, just to have Claudia to drive, but it's what I wanted. No more taxis. We could go out when we wanted and come back when we wanted and we did that week. Castle, cinema, park, my mum's town... I didn't cry when they left, but boy did I cry the night before. Luckily Giona was asleep, so he didn't witness his dad crying.

I regularly went out, on my own, but it was getting colder. I went down to the seafront and while I was there I saw the local Council moving the beach huts, in preparation for winter and the storms it can bring. It was funny seeing all the beach huts, so tightly huddled together.

Because it was getting colder, I bought some windproof, fleecy gloves and a thin, bright yellow, windproof jacket from an auction web site.

My fleecy gloves came, soon followed by my bright yellow, wind-proof jacket. It was so bright, fluorescent yellow actually. With regard to the gloves, I initially ordered a medium, but the seller contacted me via the auction web site and only had large left. I hit on an idea, so when the large gloves arrived, which I ordered, I instructed the carers to immediately wash them on a hot wash and put on a hot dry. It was a gamble that paid off, as the gloves shrunk to a medium large, otherwise as the seller said (I e-mailed him) "I might end up with gloves for a doll". The gloves and jacket certainly kept the chilly wind off.

I eventually heard from the hospital specialist, who commented on my level of activity and assured me that it was safe for me to stop wearing the TED stockings and, in his view, I wouldn't need an alternative, because of my level of activity. I was taking daily aspirin, along with a garlic capsule and I had some special oil put on my bisc-weet each morning, of which I had one, followed by marmalade on toast, which changed to just yeast extract spread, no butter, as I was dieting, a chopped up kiwi fruit and three orange and cranberry juices to drink, during which we were asked what we wanted for lunch, out of a vegetarian dish, an ordinary dish or an omelette. Sometimes I chose the vegetarian option, or had an omelette if I didn't fancy what was being offered. There was no choice at tea apart from sandwiches, if you didn't like what was being offered. I stopped having coffee some months before, primarily because of the sugar, even though the juice I replaced it with probably had a higher sugar content and secondly because I would cough more with coffee. I coughed with juice, but not as much. The oil, garlic and aspirin all had blood-thinning qualities, which would help prevent me from further strokes and prevent thrombosis, so I wasn't worried. I had my TED stockings for about a year, so I was glad when they were thrown out. Now they were gone, it meant I could wear shorts in the summer months.

My key worker changed again, as my old one had more responsibilities given to her. I didn't mind, as I quite often sought this carer out when she was on shift.

It was lucky I bought that fluorescent yellow coat. I went out one day and the chair cut out on the promenade, which had some sand on it, about two miles from the home. I didn't know at the time that it had a safety cut out switch, I was told that later. I was so embarrassed. I phoned the home and they were able to understand the communication aid. I told them of my predicament and where I was and two carers came to rescue me. It was the weekend, a Sunday afternoon to be precise, so it was very busy. It was a nice day, sunny, but cold, no wind to speak of, just a slight breeze. I sat there in my fluorescent yellow jacket, waiting to be rescued. The two carers that came, girls, only spotted me because of "THAT" jacket. They put the chair on manual and I was eventually pushed out of the sandy bit.

The girls wheeled me to a safe place, out of the wind, even though I wasn't cold, as I pointed out the jacket and gloves were windproof. Then they realised they couldn't get me in their car. The owner of the home was in a meeting and it would be some time before he was free, and the maintenance man-cum-driver was half way round, getting his shopping. So I told the girls they could use my car. So I was put in a shelter, to keep the breeze off that I couldn't feel, and they went off to get my car. They soon returned in my car and wheeled me in, but I had to instruct them on how to anchor me down and strap me in. We got back to the home and I was wheeled out the car and into the building, where I was ceremoniously pushed to my room. As I couldn't move, tea that night was in my room. The table that was in my room was manoeuvred between the front wheels of my chair. I watched a lot of television that afternoon and evening.

The following morning I didn't bother with breakfast. The Manager had phoned up the suppliers of my new chair and they could deliver it that morning. Suddenly it didn't matter that my chair had broken down, I was getting my new one. I didn't have to wait too long before it was silently brought in, it was so quiet. It looked great. I had to be hoisted in and out of it a few times, so the engineer could get it right for me. Eventually he was finished. I was mobile again. I have to admit, it was very difficult to control. It was so sensitive. Even on gear one it was faster than my old one and there were another four to go! I crashed frequently and the first three gears were eventually adjusted, to make it easier to control. As it was slightly longer and wider, corners and doorways were approached and negotiated with caution.

It came with a headrest, but I seldom used it, only to push myself back, as I used the headrest for leverage and for sunbathing in the summer months.

The Manager advised me to keep the old chair as a back up, as it was allocated to me for as long as I needed it anyway.

During a meeting it was decided that perhaps I would be more comfortable on a profile bed – that's an electric one, to the layman, you can change position in so many different ways and that a record be kept, only in the day, until the new bed arrived, of my reason for calling. The idea was it would prepare me for the outside world (as that was the plan) and give the powers that be an idea of my needs, outside of mealtimes, where personal care would be catered for, if I needed it and I should go to bed at TEN when the bed arrived, as that is about the latest I could stay up in the community. That was going to take some change, I can tell you, as I was a night owl, not going to bed until one o'clock in the morning sometimes. I could watch television, if I wanted.

Conveens were the answer, as carers wouldn't need to visit me so often and it would give me more independence, in case I was to go out for any length of time, which I did, when it was warmer, whereas I would be tied more if I used the bottle. I wanted big capacity bags that would hold 1500 millilitres. These, I was told, would only be available if I went into the community. I was only upgraded to 750 millilitre bags.

I cleaned my teeth every morning now, before breakfast, as that was part of the new regime I was on. Previously I had cleaned them after breakfast. I cleaned them before breakfast and just before I went to bed. I didn't have water on my toothbrush, nor did I spit into a cup, most of the toothpaste fell out anyway, which is why I had a towel draped round my neck.

I regularly went on estate agent web sites, hunting for a suitable property, ideally a two bedroom property I was told later. I found lots of suitable one bedroom properties, but two bedroom proved to be harder.

I sold that bright yellow windproof jacket, as it was a struggle for the carers to put on. I put it on an auction web site and it was soon sold to a keen cyclist, I found out through correspondence. I got a better one that was lined and in red and the carers could put on easier.

At least I wasn't bright yellow now when I went out, just bright red.

I ordered some ladies' weights off the internet and when they arrived, just before Christmas, the stand was assembled and the maintenance man was able to find a very small table, for them to stand on, so I could get to them. I am guessing, but I think the small table was the smallest one, originally from a nest of tables. I used the weights on my left arm Mondays, Wednesdays and Fridays. I was quite sure it would take a long time before I saw any significant benefit. I could barely use the weights, they were so heavy to me. I was disappointed in myself, as previously, before my strokes, I had been able to use quite heavy dumbbells. These were so light and for some exercises I didn't even use any weight. Still, you have got to start somewhere I suppose. I was still quite lean, I hadn't wasted away at all, just not as defined as I was before I had my strokes.

It didn't take too long before my bed arrived and after a short period of adjustment, I soon started my new regime of going to bed at ten o'clock and if I called through the night it was to be written down on a chart the Manager had prepared for me and it was to be kept in my room. The bed was great, it raised up and down, the head raised up, the feet went up, it sat you up and also bent your knees, I could just press the control pad. The mattress was quite comfortable as well. I could easily watch television from my bed now and it had a monkey bar that I could use. I wasn't able to pull myself right up, only about a millimetre or so, but it took the weight off and that was enough to adjust my top half, or drag myself up the bed, if I had slid down a bit. Anyway, it encouraged me to strengthen my left arm, I had to raise the leg bit, so that gravity helped me manoeuvre myself up the bed, which I achieved fraction by fraction. I slept quite well in it, not really waking through the night now.

I had a new conveen each morning, but as I discovered I only received ten leg bags a month, I tried to make them last three days, even though some of the carers wanted to throw them out each night, when it was taken off and after I had pulled the conveen off, which didn't hurt, just stretched me a little. It looked painful, but it wasn't. If I ran out, as they came in boxes of thirty and it might come off in the day and need replacing, or the carers would need another one, as the first one wasn't put on correctly, "Cock-ups" I would call them (excuse the pun), I would wear a pad or just use the bottle, it depended on whether I needed to go out or not.

There was very rarely a film on the box, so I spent a fortune on DVDs. I am sure I became the local DVD shop's most regular customer. Jacob loved going for rides on the bed, him and any other child he came with or who happened to be visiting.

I loved music, any, so I ordered some very powerful speakers off the internet. When they arrived I was very keen that they should replace my cheap ones. The quality was so good, even on low volume, but when they were turned up it was something else. I didn't even have them turned up to their full potential. I described them as "bringing my music to life".

I heard sounds I hadn't heard before. And they had a separate volume and bass control, which sat on the desk, next to my laptop and I could control it. I always had my music so loud, I liked it loud and as it was linked to my computer and I was on top of it, it sounded even louder still. I would close the door of course, which I could manage in my wheelchair, as it was on a floor catch that I could hit and then the door would automatically close. Even when I wrote, I found the loud music helped me concentrate rather than it being a distraction.

It was close to Christmas, one month away, in fact, and I made a decision to get all my Christmas things from an auction website. There was the post and packaging to pay, but they were generally cheaper and the choice was endless. I bought so much and Christmas paper and tags, I even bought myself a three foot, ready decorated, fibre optic Christmas tree. I bought Claudia's locally, a gold and topaz bracelet.

The presents seemed to arrive every day for about a month, when the paper arrived, I think I had enough for the next two Christmases, let alone this one! As well as buying both my key worker and the Manager a plant each, I wrote and dedicated a poem to each of them:

Thank you, Jackie
For all you do
All that wrapping
And the Christmas cards too!

You do my post
Whenever I ask
I give you the most
Incredible task!

Unwrapping my parcels
I seem to get every day
"I don't want to cut Tim's nails"
I hear you say!

At lunch, I always gesture small
You always say big
I know your only joking
And with me you like to kid!

As my key worker
You give me your time
I appreciate that
There are others to see, you are not just mine!

So, thanks again
For what you do
Happy New Year
And Best Wishes for your family and YOU

And for the Manager;

You make calls for me
And take calls for me
Fight for me
Explain to me

Speaking is not easy
And you may not see what you do
Affects me deep within
But inside I do say thank you

You've cared for me
Comforted me
Listened to me
Worried about me

I see your individuality
Your personality is laid bare
Caring, kind and considerate
Passionate and fair

You have advised me
Been fair to me
Encouraged me
Taken notes for me

I know that I can't be easy at times
And my stubbornness shows through
But you always talk to me calmly
You know just what to do

The Best That I Can Be

Written for me
Just helped me
Smiled at me
Laughed with me
For all that you do
I hold you most dear
So, Merry Christmas and a Happy New Year!

CHAPTER NINETEEN

My car had to be taken up to Bristol Airport, as Claudia and Giona were due to fly in and as it was Boxing Day, there was no public transport, so I asked my two comical friends if they could take my car up and leave it in the car park for her. They said "Yes"

The children loved their presents, in fact everyone did. I was quite thoughtful. I bought a play suit for Giona. It was far, far to big for him. He looked ridiculous, it did cause some laughs, between me and Claudia. He liked it though. It was a blue suit and mask, as blue was his favourite colour. It was one of those suits from a children's television series, where there is a small group of youngsters that automatically change into these colourful "Heroes" and fight the most ridiculous, evil monsters that eventually change into big ridiculous evil monsters. The "Heroes" combine to create a big robot thingy that always saves the day. Give me the old puppet heroes that fly futuristic craft any day of the week! There was nothing ridiculous about that...

We opened the presents the day after Boxing Day, as Claudia and Giona didn't arrive until ten on Boxing Day night and Jacob wasn't due to arrive until the following morning. After all the presents had been opened, we went to my sister's the next day and opened some more. It was very tricky entering there, although they had some long telescopic, aluminium ramps, which they had hired. I don't know how many steps there were, maybe just three or four. I thought the last step was scary, which was at least a foot high. I was wrong. The ramps were above the last step and I had to inch myself forward, until a seesaw effect happened and the ramps went down and just reached the final step. I was in, thank God. Getting out was the opposite, but I had to go down backwards, as it was thought that was the safest way. I got stuck many times and I had visions of the fire brigade being called and doing, something, God knows what. But I got out and lived to tell the tale, but it's a tale I would rather forget and that wasn't it for the excitement. Because it was a bitterly cold evening, as the car turned on to the road, for my sister lived in the middle of a cow field, the car got stuck on some ice. Eventually, Claudia, who was not used to driving in these conditions, as she was from the city, managed to inch the car back off the ice and then was able to drive forward, avoiding the ice. What an evening! We did eat some nice food and I had some alcohol, which I needed. It was thick and creamy, Irish cream liquor and about the only alcoholic beverage I could drink, as all the others were too thin and made me cough.

Claudia, the boys and me went out nearly every day. Although it was Christmas, it wasn't too cold out. We all ate out on New Year's Eve and after we had finished, we went into a dedicated play area that was attached to the restaurant. It went up and up, it was too big for Giona really and Claudia was worried he might get hurt. As it was mainly soft and I knew he wouldn't hurt himself, I told her not to be concerned and to let him get on with it. Jacob and the bigger boys would look after him, anyway.

The boys had fun in there until closing time and anxious Claudia and relaxed me were there waiting to greet them when they were finished.

We didn't really see the New Year in, as we were too busy talking. When Claudia was here, the home turned a blind eye to me going to bed at ten. Of course, that wouldn't happen in the community, I would have to go to bed at ten, but then we would all have our own rooms.

It was late one day, dark, not late at night, just late in the afternoon, anyway, the boys, Claudia and me all piled in the car and went to buy some special fish that I wanted: loaches that would eat the algae in the fish tank. I subsequently lost one called "Suck". "Blow" was okay and lived up to his name attacking all the other fish, I had names for them too, but I won't go into that. Doesn't everybody name their fish, or was I just sad? Where was I? Oh yes, buying two loaches... I couldn't get in the shop, as there was a rather large step, so I just waited outside in the cold darkness and the drizzle. I also wanted five weeds to replace the artificial glow in the dark ones I had (was that sad too?). As I couldn't get in the shop, I left the choosing up to Claudia. I think she got stressed a little, what with me "beeping" every five minutes to see where she was and Giona wanting to buy me a dragon, which he subsequently dropped and broke, which was later stuck back together by the maintenance man and put in the fish tank to scare the fish. I wouldn't dare say I was getting cold, in case it just pushed Claudia over the edge (but I was).

It was soon time for Claudia and Giona to go and I cried a few days before in the car. Luckily, we had dropped Jacob at his mum's and Giona was asleep, so again he didn't see his Dad crying, which was sure to upset him. I didn't cry the morning they left, but I did cry much later.

The Manager came and consoled me and offered me some nursing wipes. I don't know when I was to see them again, as it was expensive for Claudia to keep coming here, as there were the flights for two of them, time off work and all the expenses associated with coming here.

I built up a reputation for being witty and intelligent, although I have no idea where the latter came from. Like writing this, I have no idea how I had the ability to write. Maybe it was always there and the strokes just bought it out. At least, I think I can write.

Claudia never took that play suit, as we did both agree it was just a little bit too big for him. I would buy another, slightly smaller and send it on.

I did play on my condition a bit, for a while, in any correspondence, when I bought anything on auction, web sites on the internet, I always pointed out my plight. Why, I don't really know. When I went out, vehicles would often stop for me, allowing me to cross the road and I would nod my head in recognition of them stopping. Shopkeepers got to know me and were particularly courteous, as was everybody I came across, even children. Once I was stopped by a foreign student, who asked me directions to a certain employment agency. I knew where it was, so typed out some directions on the communication aid. I must admit, at first, I thought he had a flyer to give me, or he wanted me to fill in a questionnaire. I was very surprised he stopped me.

After Claudia and Giona went back, there was one day when I seriously contemplated suicide. I had it all worked out, I would go down to the chemist the next day, as it was late, ask for two pots of their own painkillers, get them to open one, come back, hide the open one under my t-shirt and get one of the carers to open the other one. I had had enough that day it was just too much, my condition, not being a proper father, not being in Rome and not being next to Claudia. I sent the most horrible, worrying text to Claudia. She phoned the home and phoned me. She talked to me for a while and told me I was being selfish and stupid.

The next day I woke up and felt better about life and besides, I had forgotten what I was supposed to do.

It took me ages to find a smaller playsuit for Giona, but I did. It had to be a blue one as well. It was slightly different, but more up to date. It had a muscle chest, like the other one.

I keep remembering things to write and keep darting back to previous chapters, before I forget. I go as far back as the beginning. It's so difficult remembering which chapter to go to, to put in what I have remembered. But I do. Chapters started off so small, but they have grown, since I have remembered things. I am still typing this with one finger mainly, by the way, sometimes two, but mainly my middle finger on my left hand. My index finger is hard to straighten out. It does straighten, but it is now naturally bent and my left arm that does the typing drags on the edge of my laptop. I cannot hold it up, as that would be too tiring for me. Sometimes my arm shoots off the edge and I press the wrong letter. It has taken me about eighteen months to write this far, I anticipate about another three. I will tell you at the end.

I don't write every day, sometimes I do, it depends how I feel. Sometimes I get blocked, as I have already said. Sometimes words and memories just pour out. Other times I can't think of anything. Sometimes typing is just too difficult for me, as my arm feels too heavy.

A little bit more about my condition. Apart from being labile which can be very annoying at times, as I smile easily and smile if it's good or bad, so it confuses people. Sure, I genuinely smile, but as I said, I smile too easily. You know my left arm is weak; it varies on a day to day basis. I can only lift it above my head if I am lying down. If I am sitting in my chair, it takes all my effort to lift it up to the top of my head. Drinking is a problem, as I keep thinking I will drop it or cough. My right arm is permanently bent at the elbow and I constantly wear a hand splint, to stop my hand forming a fist. At night, I wear an arm splint, to try and straighten my arm out. I only wear it at night, as it would be too awkward to go around all day with a straight arm. I would feel like one of those things on wheels, that went round saying "*Exterminate, exterminate*". There's barely no movement to speak of, though both arms are capable of gripping and pulling me up on the Standaid, without the belt on, but ask me to bend my fingers in on my right hand and I can't do it.

My head hangs. I can hold it up with ease, but it's more comfortable if I hang my head slightly. I get spasms in my head and it turns to the left mainly when I get them, which is quite often. On occasions, through the day, I also get an itch on my head and because I have such a sensitive scalp, this causes me to shake viol7ently, which can be quite a problem if I am holding a drink, as there's no prior warning. Some mornings it interfered with my breakfast. It is a problem when it is washed or brushed. It doesn't really hurt, it's just so sensitive.

You know my legs don't work, although there is a little movement in each. More so in my left leg, which I can bend a little. I can't bend my right leg, and I get clonus – that's an involuntary, rhythmic, shaking of the leg, it bounces up and down. I mainly get it in my right leg, but my left gets it on occasions. I get it a lot when my feet are put on the Standaid, or when they're first put on the footplates of the wheelchair.

You can stop it by lifting the leg, just under the knee. Although everybody is told to press down on the knee, I have found lifting to be more effective. Should I get it when no one's around, I use all my concentration and push down with my legs. This stops it.

I cannot shout, but I can scream. Most people now can understand about 95% of what I say, so long as I keep it to one word. If it's longer, I take a breath between each word, as I have discovered I not only say words clearer, but it is much more discernible for the listener. But I am keen to become more articulate and my sense of humour is drier now.

Oh, have you ever tried highlighting on the computer with one hand? It's so difficult, even more so for me, as my fingers don't stretch or work properly. Try it, see how you get on.

There was one carer, I think she was the oldest, at sixty. She was always pulling my leg, but in a nice way. She wanted the best for me. Anyway, I was always teasing her. I got some ginseng from the Chinese acupuncturist, in little 10 millilitre bottles you pierced with a straw. He didn't speak English very well. I didn't really know what it did, I think it helped stimulate the nerves. The acupuncturist did tell me once, but I had forgotten. I probably didn't understand him anyway. She called it "gnat's piss" and it stuck. Soon everybody knew what it was. I had the "gnat's piss" twice a day, if I remembered.

She hated the word "allocated" and what it meant, so I made up a special notice and gave it to her:

ALLOCATION ERROR

Due to an allocation error, a job you were allocated to do, hasn't been allocated. This was due to an allocation error in the allocation process. The job should have been allocated to you some time ago, but due to the error in allocation you weren't allocated. The job is allocated to you because you are the most suitable person to have it allocated to.

Allocating is the simplest way of allocating a job.

The Management thought long and hard before allocating it to you, but now that you are allocated the job, it is felt that you will shine at it. We are sorry we overlooked your allocation, we thought you had been automatically allocated the job. It has taken sometime to find out that the job you should have been allocated to wasn't in fact allocated. The Management didn't pick up on the allocation, as they thought you were automatically allocated by the allocation process. From time to time, the automatic allocation process does break down and you are not allocated. We didn't envisage this. All allocating will be done manually in future, as we now don't trust the automatic allocation system, as it has happened before, with a senior carer being allocated to clear up Andrew's saliva, as he has a habit of spitting. (Andrew is the Chef)

Allocation of a senior carer was wrong, it should have been allocated to just a carer. So, as you can see, the automatic allocation doesn't allocate correctly at times.

Once again, apologies for the automatic allocation system not allocating you. Be assured that you are now allocated and please accept our heartfelt gratitude for what you do here and now hope the job of Chief Shit Shoveller, which you are now allocated, is in itself just reward and we only wish you had been allocated it sooner.

She laughed so much. I gave it to her whilst she was with all the other carers. They gathered round, while she read it out. It wasn't long before all the others got her a faeces sample collector of her own.

The acupuncture didn't hurt, even though I resembled a pin cushion. In China they always recommend it to stroke victims. I read on the internet it was best to have it about three months after you had a stroke. I started having it at over one year. Maybe I was too late, who knows?

CHAPTER TWENTY

You know, as I come more and more up to date, I just can't think of anything to write. You would have thought it would be easier, but it is not, it is harder. Ask me what happened a year ago, it is so vivid, but ask me to write about an incident that happened recently, I remember so little. Maybe it is my stroke or maybe it is because I am getting older. I can't blame everything on the strokes, or can I?

The T-bar seemed to sink in more into my new bed, more so than the old one and when the weight of my legs were on it, it was squashed down even more, hardly lifting my knees up at all, so I decided I would be better if I had the size I had at Rowans, I guessed it was the next size up. So I went along to see the Manager, so she could order one for me. Well, when it arrived, it was so big, someone had got it wrong, as it was definitely not the next size up. It resembled a miniature submarine. Needless to say, it was the subject of many jokes with the carers. I tried it and kept it.

I was asked if I wanted to join the local speech therapy group. I said yes. It was every other week at the local hospital. It was only for an hour and a half and attended by some who went to the Stroke Group. Only about six went to this one, with the emphasis being on verbal communication and gestures. Sometimes I would verbally communicate, other times I would use my communication aid. We would talk about all sorts of topics, then if there was time, we would play hangman, then it was time to be loaded into the ambulance, which not only collected me and one other, but also took us there.

One morning my key worker asked me if I minded being put on the bed and taken off again, as she was being assessed and her assessor was coming in to do this. I said I didn't mind. When they came in later that morning, I had something prepared in my communication aid: "Don't take the piss and make me laugh." This was said in front of her assessor, who found it funny, so did my key worker.

I was always writing things on my laptop, for the Manager or carers. If it wasn't notes for my condition, it was messages that were too long for my communication aid or it was me trying to be funny. One carer was very accident prone and talked a lot. I suggested she attend night school for her condition, but of course there was no such place that did one – or was there?:

Enroll now for the combined Incessant talking and accident prone course

Because we have found that most people who talk a lot are inherently clumsy

It's a 10 week course that commences after the Easter break.

I mean holiday, as break is not a word that should be used.

During that 10 weeks, we will try and cover the following:

(So long as the lecturer is concentrating on his driving and not jibbering away to his passenger, causing him to crash)

Week 1—Why am I here, when I could be at home doing something more constructive?

Week 2—Accidents. Why they always happen to me.

Week 3—Why am I so clumsy and is there anything I can do?—Group discussion.

Week 4—Why do I talk such crap?

Week 5—How not to talk the hind leg off a donkey.—Role play.

Week 6—Accents. Do they make me more boring?

The Best That I Can Be

Week 7—Can I change my life and be like other people, or is it too late?—Group discussion.

Week 8—How to cover up accidents as they happen.

Week 9—Does being clumsy make me attractive to the opposite sex?—Group discussion.

Week 10—Has this helped, or is there no hope for me?

Professor Ivan Slippup will be your lecturer, he's Welsh but don't let that put you off!

Lectures will run for 2 hours, 7pm till 9pm, with a coffee break, sorry, drinks interval halfway(that's after an hour for those of you that find halfway difficult to understand).

Any queries or for enrolment, please contact the central office.

It is anticipated this will be the only one, as Ivan is returning to Wales to sing in a male voice choir and no one else would be mad enough to do it!

It took me about two hours to think it all up, I was able to give it to her before she went off shift that day. She took it all the way it was meant to be taken, anyway "her conditions" had been pointed out to her by her partner and family.

About a week later, I wrote her another one, aimed at her stupidity (there's no other way to put it). She was always forgetting things, getting things wrong, running over her foot and crashing my chair, when she parked it in my room at night, so I wrote her another note, on the same theme as the other one:

Back by popular demand the "Daft as a brush course"

Enroll now, as we anticipate a great demand. The course will run after Easter for 10 weeks.

Week 1. Is my condition inherited and can I pass it on to my children? On-going project.

Week 2. Is it limited to blondes or can some brunettes get it as well?

Week 3. How do other people see me?—Group discussion.

Week 4. Daft or stupid. What's the difference?

Week 5. Why do they say "Daft as a brush" anyway?

Week 6. How can I remember things?—Group discussion.

Week 7. How to fool the opposite sex and other people.

Week 8. Can I change?

Week 9. Is there a link between being daft, clumsiness and talking incessantly?

Week 10.   Project analysis then down the pub!

Because of the high demand of this course it shall run again and again and again and again... Refreshment breaks are not written down, as most will forget anyway. Same as role play, we don't do any, as students forget what they're doing. It will run from 7pm to 9pm, day to be decided, but we will try not to clash with other courses you may be on. SAVE MONEY. Why not do 2 different courses and save 25%?

She took it well—again.

CHAPTER TWENTY-ONE

Shhh... I managed to get hold of some cannabis. I had read on various web sites that it not only helped pain (which I wasn't in) but also helped with spasms (which I did get). Anyway, just for medicinal purposes I took some and for personal use, just in case any police are reading this. I couldn't smoke it, so I ate it. I kept it under a jumper, in a drawer I don't really use, although I do use it now. I told Claudia and she suggested, just to be on the safe side, I tell one carer that I was going to take it. I confided to one carer; she didn't mind and thought it was a good idea anyway. It relaxed me, I think it helped my spasms, but who cares anyway? I took it just before the carers came and put me to bed. It took about one hour to take effect, so I wasn't high when I was put to bed. When I went to bed, I would watch a film. The film had to be very, very stimulating, or the cannabis would relax me so much I would fall asleep. Eating it had one major drawback: what goes in must come out and when I went on the toilet, it would smell so much, but there was nothing I could do about it. How incriminating. I just hope that whoever got me off the toilet didn't recognise the smell.

Just before Christmas I had an eye test in the home, which was unusual, as previously I had gone to the hospital for my eye appointments. Anyway, my eyes were tested and it was recommended I have bifocals. Even though I could see quite well in the distance, these would be much better than my very cheap ones for reading and computer work and make me see better for medium distance and things that were about four foot to about sixteen foot away. I chose some very light, purple, half frames. When they arrived, I forgot just how light they were. They took a bit of adjusting to get them to fit, as I was forever pushing them up my nose, as they kept slipping, but eventually I got them just right. For things further away than sixteen foot, I would pull them down my nose anyway, as my eyesight at that distance and more, was better without the glasses. They didn't take time for me to adjust to them, nor did I get headaches, which a carer told me I would probably get.

I particularly liked the weekend as I didn't go on the bike then in the evenings, which was my choice. I gave myself weekends off, so it gave me much more time to write. No session was ever long enough though, unless I was "blocked", which did happen on occasion.

I got wet feet about moving into my own place. I thought it was better for me here: they knew me, my needs would be catered for, there was someone here 24 hours a day, whereas in my own place carers would only be in four times a day to get me up and see to my breakfast, lunch, tea and to put me to bed. I would always get physiotherapy here, as I don't know if I could afford it, when I get my own place. I felt safe, no bills, I was sure I would be encouraged more here, I liked the area and I could contribute financially to Jacob and Giona. Then the social worker (oh, that's what they do) came to see me and spelt out all the plus points of moving out. I saw some, but I was a bit blinkered when I worked it out. She said the children would grow and what then, where would they stay? I hadn't thought of that. In about two to three years, my personal money, which I had to use to stay at Oldway, would run out. Oldway cost about £520 a week. It was doubtful if I could contribute to Jacob's and Giona's welfare, I hadn't thought of that either. I would be investing my hard earned money for Jacob and Giona or their children, got me on that one too. I would have more room, the furniture didn't have to be donated from shops, which might be cheap and cheerful, I could buy it myself, if I could afford to and I could ask family and friends. I would be entitled to more benefits and grants. True, I would be on my own more, but in their experience I would gain even more independence.

I started looking again on the internet that night.

I was always having a joke with the carers. One morning I was asked to guess the age of the two carers that were taking me for a shower, one was my key worker, I guessed her age was about forty. She took umbrage at that, as she was only late thirties. Thank God I didn't have to guess the age of the other one, as she readily told me her age. I went to the local chemist soon after and gave my key worker some anti-aging cream.

Her eldest daughter, at nearly eighteen, had an accident on a dry ski slope, she ended up breaking her arm. Her mum, my key worker, ended up doing everything for her, even bathing her, she told me. I saw this as a golden opportunity to write something. So I did:

An Idiot's Guide To A Dry Ski Slope

1. Remember your skis. It's a bit difficult to ski without them. Although one bloody idiot tried.

2. Please take your skis off when you go. Apart from being hard to walk in them, you look a bloody idiot and it's difficult to sit in the car, let alone drive it.

3. Try to ski down not up. As well as being difficult, it causes accidents.

4. We are not up in the mountains, so dress accordingly.

5. We don't have snow, so snowball fights or building a snowman are out of the question.

6. No matter how good you are, please don't build any ski jumps or slaloms.

7. It's not Ski Sunday, so don't expect any cameras.

8. We don't have the facilities for a toboggan run or sledging, or the luge, for that matter.

9. You can urinate in the snow, but you can't on a dry ski slope. Please use the toilet facilities provided.

10. There's no off piste section, so you don't have to look out for trees.

11. Try not to ski over people. As this is very bumpy and uncomfortable for the person you ski over.

12. Above all, try not to fall over, as you might hurt yourself, or worse still, break or fracture something, like an arm and your mum will end up doing everything for you, like having a bath!

Please remember the management take no responsibilities for bloody idiots and if you are stupid enough to have an accident please enter it in the "I'm a bloody idiot" book. If you're stupid enough that your accident prevents you from writing, get a representative to do it for you.

Apparently it went down well. Her mum liked it anyway.

I was very disappointed with my new chair. It was meant to be top of the range, but I found everything was forever coming loose. The maintenance man was constantly tightening things up, especially the footplates. I could understand it if I constantly went over rough terrain, but I didn't, it was the middle of winter and I stayed in most of the time, working on this. It was comfortable though, more so than the old one, which I kept as a backup, on the Manager's advice. I was very grateful I kept it, because as it was narrower than my new chair, it would fit in the car better, so I would swap into it whenever Claudia was here, or if I was to go in the car.

At Christmas I bought some Irish cream liqueur. I chose a cheaper brand than the original I had at my sister's. I thought it would be the same, but it wasn't—so much for me being cost conscious. It was stronger than the original and too strong for me, it made me cough and splutter. Mixed with ice cream it was okay. So I had it every night, poured over ice cream, which I would wait to melt, then suck it up through a straw.

If you think "Mmm, that sounds nice, I must try it tonight". a word of warning: although it's delicious with ice cream, don't have it with sorbet, it congeals.

My brother sent me a microphone, from Canada, for my laptop. I got it plugged in, so now I could not only see him, but I could attempt to talk to him as well, which he generally understood.

My speech was getting better, or were people just getting used to my voice? Once three carers came in my room, it slips my mind why they came in, but they did. I verbally told them two jokes and they understood, they were quite short and most of the time, I told it word by word.

What were they? Okay: "How do you make a dog drink? Put in a liquidiser." and "How do you find a foxhole? … Lift its tail up." My favourite one though was one I had told some months before, on my communication aid: "How do you get rid of unwanted pubic hair? … Take it out of your teeth." Sorry about that one, but I guess you were curious.

I went down to the health shop one day. It wasn't the usual lady. I verbally said: oil, honey, zinc and some garlic tablets, which she understood. Okay, my voice must be getting better, so credit where it's due, NO, no credit, I can do better.

In the dining room now, nearly all the walking sticks were safely placed, so they didn't fall down and give me a fright. The chap next to me "Squeaky" always told me when he was moving his chair (or he told me just after he started moving it, which was too late then, lucky I watched him out the corner of my eye). Due to his condition, he couldn't move the chair properly and it abruptly scraped on the wooden floor. Whatever I was doing, eating or drinking, I would stop and wait for him to move out and go, before I would resume.

My nights were going well. I didn't really use the bell now, though I must say it took some getting used to. If I am caught short, I can use the bottle, although I had one or two accidents to start off with. There is a lid on the bottle, so it's quite safe, it stays under the covers, next to me, until the morning. It is my choice that the conveen is not on at night, as it makes me feel more normal without it.

This time was going to be a long haul without Claudia and not seeing Giona, as they were not due to fly over until Easter. They don't have a half-term in Italy. Christmas until Easter that's a long time.

I would quite often refer to e-mails I sent to Claudia now (I often e-mailed her), as they jogged my memory for what to write, as I always told her everything that went on.

I sent them a box of goodies, DVDs, a cuddly toy that spoke amongst other things. Oh, and a replacement play suit for Giona, his size this time. It was packed up and sent by my key worker, who I always kept busy.

Claudia was very concerned about me leaving here. She e-mailed me with her concerns, I sent one back:

I definitely won't share. Where would u, g and j stay? I am sorry, but that would just destroy me. I am so used to u sleeping here now. That would seem like going backwards. Sorry.

I can't choose who's next door, I can only choose what's for sale, that might be near someone or not.

I can't slow down the buying. The council has money available from April. If I don't choose now, they will be suspicious of me, as there are properties on the market and they will start charging me for staying, that's £520 a week.

If I am nearer to Exeter like Newton Abbot, I can go swimming there.

I am thinking what's best for me, short and long term.

I think moving out will be a challenge, both physically and men- tally. I am not afraid of that. I am ready. it will be financially just as hard here in 2/3 years, when all my money has gone.

It would kill me staying here if my family can't stay with me, because I have 2 big boys, they won't be little for long.

I am thinking of myself, my family is very important to me.

Physically I may be better off here, but mentally, which will affect me physically, I think I would do better in my own place.

Sure I was concerned for moving out, in case I needed someone. I would have an emergency alarm round my neck, but I think it would be better in the long run. As I said, Jacob and Giona wouldn't be little boys forever, where would they stay here when they got bigger? Anyway, Jacob may choose to live with me when he is older. It was important to me that my family could always be with me and like any parent, I want to be able to pass something on, financially, to my children, or their children, when I eventually go. I would put what I could to a property and the council would top it up. It was in my interest to contribute what I could, there was no mortgage to pay on what they gave, but they would always own the percentage they put in. There was no way of hiding my money, what's mine is mine, no matter where it is, or who's got it.

CHAPTER TWENTY-TWO

I hunted around for some wheelchair insurance in case I crashed, or worse still, knocked over an old granny, whilst I am blasting along the seafront at full belt. Eight miles per hour doesn't seem fast in comparison to what you do in your car, but it is fast enough, when you're dodging pedestrians. I could easily run into someone or knock them over. If it was very busy, I used to crawl along at the same pace of whoever was in front of me, until I could pass them safely, then if it was all clear, I used to open her up again. Although the wheelchair had five gears, I was always on gear three on ordinary width pavements. One day I was in a park, going down hill, the path was wet and I found my driving skills were taking me close to a wall, I abruptly stopped, so I could correct my direction, but the momentum was too much and I skidded, luckily, into a bush, that was growing out from the wall. No damage done and I wasn't hurt, except for my pride. I had to do battle with the bush though, as it was hampering my access to the chair controls. I went on, very cautiously. Just goes to show what can happen and why you need insurance. Thank goodness for that bush!

As I said, two bedroom, wheelchair-friendly properties are very hard to come by, but I found one though, it was in the local council's catchment area and at a price I could afford. The location wasn't brilliant, mind, but beggars can't be choosers. I hassled the estate agents for what seemed like weeks, so I could get a viewing, but on one of their many e-mails they said that the viewing was proving difficult, due to the hours that the vendor kept (I think he was a practicing vampire). Eventually, it was taken off the market and my heart sank as I was back at square one. Would something suitable *ever* crop up?

One of the two girls that organised the daily activities and outings for the residents, which I always declined, much to her amusement, I was so fiercely independent, mentioned to me that I could go swimming each week, well go for a float, as far as I was concerned. I was very interested as I used to go when I was at Rowans, if you remember. I ordered some swimming shorts from the auction web site and I received them just before the next week, when I was due to go for a "float" for the first time. Getting changed was a laugh, as I was physically held up and supported by two helpers and my legs would quite often collapse, giving them more weight to worry about. Thank goodness I only weighed about twelve stone (hopefully slightly less). Then I was physically transferred into a special wheelchair, that could be hoisted up and lowered into the pool, then I was just slid off. I eventually went down to one float, which went under me and resembled a long bit of pipe. I had originally started off with three floats, as that is what I had when I was at Rowans. I would try and flap my good arm in the water and the helpers would try and loosen my legs and after a while my legs would loosen a little bit, but they were still tight. I was dragged around the pool for just under an hour and that was swimming, or floating, as I called it.

I was chuffed to bits when I e-mailed what I had done of this story to a publisher for his honest comments. Imagine my surprise when he e-mailed me back about three hours later and said he just had to keep reading it and found it "Compelling" and he would love the chance to publish it when it was finished and he wouldn't change it. I was so emotional, I am even emotional now as I write this. I cried with happiness, I just couldn't believe it, he was the first one that I contacted, I never dreamt it would be that easy. Yes, I thought it would be published, but I anticipated a struggle to find a publisher. I had given what I had done to family and friends and they said it was fantastic, but I just thought they were being biased and I took what they said with a pinch of salt, so to speak. I guess time will tell. Claudia was so thrilled when I managed to say "Publisher" over the phone.

I was having problems with my e-mail. I told a friend who was not only "into" computers, but worked with them also. At first he assured me that the problem was with the recipient and not me, as it was so random, then after some further investigation he realised I did have a random e-mail problem, as he got me to do a test e-mail to everyone in my address book, I received such a small response. For weeks, it was looked into by my network provider. I don't think they even knew.

One of my fish was definitely changing colour. When I got it, it had lots of black in it and now it hardly had any. In fact, it looked quite anaemic. It didn't help that it was slightly deformed, at the back end, just before the tail. This bit was bent up. Claudia had joked that the men that sold it to me laughed and couldn't believe their luck that they had actually sold it.

I was totally addicted to buying things on the auction website. I bought so many things from there: DVD player, DVDs, nearly all my Christmas presents (and there was a lot), Easter presents including chocolate, bandanas, socks, polo shirts, trousers, shoes, jewellery, toys, razors, toothpaste, deodorant, shampoo, cotton buds, duvet covers, touch lamps – in fact, anything I wanted or didn't want, I would always look on there first. Only a couple of items went adrift in the post, for which they either sent me replacements or gave me my money back. I would recommend it to anyone; the only drawback is it's very addictive and you end up looking for and bidding for things you don't really want.

I was told it was cheaper and better to get my DVDs on the internet, from a large supermarket chain. I weighed up the pro's and con's of going with the large supermarket chain, or one of the many other ones I came across. They were all pretty similar, but I opted for one of the top ones, as the large supermarket chain wasn't classed as one of the top ones.

Me mad on Formula 1? No, apart from watching each race live, no matter what time it was on. I ordered seven Formula 1 polo shirts, off the auction site, because my wardrobe was getting low (it wasn't really, but it's a good excuse). See, I told you it had drawbacks. There was a black one, a white one, a navy blue one, a bright blue one, a bright green one, a yellow one, a grey one, I already had a red one. I got rid of some of my t-shirts, even though they were alright. Bandanas to match were a bit of a dilemma and some of them were made redundant and found their way to the back of the drawer, as they would clash with my outfit, darling.

Eventually, my laptop was rebuilt, hoping that would solve my e-mail problem, but it didn't. When it came back, a day later, as it was rebuilt by my friend, I was horrified to find that all the paragraphs and pages in this story were messed up. I had to go through it all and space out the pages and paragraphs again. The "D" drive was playing up before it was rebuilt and it was still playing up, even though it had been cleaned with a special disc cleaner I had got. My friend suggested that I get an external disc drive of the same capacity of all my programs together, which was about 40 megabytes, so that I could do a complete backup of everything on my laptop and have it safe. Yep, you guessed it again, I looked on the auction website for one. I bid many times, only to be outbid and eventually I just bought one from the auction website, as I was fed up with bidding.

The Manager approached me about swimming. I knew it wouldn't be good news and I was right. Manhandling me was against the health and safety policy, so they had to stop it, which meant I couldn't go swimming. There was another possibility, which was further away, but they had a hoist to transfer me. Thinking about it, I don't know how they would get me changed? That might still be a problem. At Rowans I was slid over to a plinth, laid down and then changed. If I could go, it wasn't due to start for about six weeks and as I am practically up to date now, I can't tell you any more.

One of the young carers was leaving and I ordered some silver charms and a charm bracelet from the auction web site again. Well, it's so cheap. Anyway, to cut a long story short, they got lost in the post. It's okay, they sent me some more, but I didn't have them for when she left, so I wrote her a quick poem, to be going on with. I say "quick" as it took me about 45 minutes;

You are going at last
Yes, you will be missed

Who will Sue go out with now
When she wants to get pissed

No more tanning with Sue
Boy, you will get pale
Very slim chance for you then
Of meeting a well matched male

All the residents will miss you
Especially your biggest fan
I don't think you will miss him though
I'm talking about Michael Seaman

No more pushing round the trolley
Dishing up the sweet
No more "personal" messes to clear up
Now that will be a treat

I am sure little Barry will miss you
(Barry was the owner, who was also quite short)
He won't be breathing down your neck
But you don't know what the bosses are like
So don't count your chickens just yet

We all wish you GOOD LUCK
No doubt you will get pissed tonight, as friends see you off
And they will all join me in saying
Why don't you ....!

She liked it and the charms and bracelet, that arrived just a few days after she had gone. I gave them to her friend to post on or give to her, when she next saw her.

I used to often dream I could walk again. They were so vivid that I would wake up the following morning believing I could. I couldn't, of course, but what did they mean? I am led to believe that they mean the opposite. Still, I can always be hopeful.

I didn't dribble half as much as I used to. I was so bad, but now I only dribble occasionally.

I was glad that winter would soon be over, as I could go out more. I seldom went out now and as my DVDs were delivered I only went out if it was really necessary, like to the bank or health shop, if I had run out of oil, honey, zinc or garlic pills. True, I had a windproof jacket and gloves, but even the windproof gloves weren't enough for my fingers, as anyone that suffers from Raynaud's and hypersensitive fingers will tell you. The bell to Oldway was a struggle at the best of times, but throw weak, cold fingers into the equation and it makes it practically impossible. Could I straighten my fingers to press that bell? No, I couldn't. I used to resort to my mobile phone and phone them up and scream when they answered. Nine times out of ten they knew it was me and where I was.

CHAPTER TWENTY-THREE

My mum had been looking for a suitable property for me and one she had overlooked because technically it was one bedroom flat came to her notice again. It had an area off the lounge, a study area, it was advertised as, as it didn't have a window, so according to building regulations, it couldn't be classed as a bedroom. Nor could it have a door, but there was nothing to stop you putting up a heavy curtain, so it could then be used as a second bedroom, which I was keen to have, so the boys had their own room. I went to see it and my mum's partner drove me over to Teignmouth to see it. It was newly converted, in an established property. I could just access it, as there was a step, but that could be rectified to make the entry and exit easier. The lounge, which you went straight into, was a good size. The kitchen was very small, but nice. It had a built-in fridge, washer/drier and attractive cooker. The bedroom was small, but I could keep my clothes in what I thought could be the second bedroom. The bathroom was small and would need converting so I could use it. It would have to be inspected by the OT that specialised in that sort of thing, but I thought it was possible. There was gas central heating, even though it seemed warm to me, as it was in-between two other flats and below another, it was decorated to a very high standard and just outside, at the front, there was a very small patio area that belonged to the flat. There was no rear garden, but there was a communal garden. I couldn't access it mind, as it had a step. It had its own, very generous parking space, immediately outside. This would need to be ramped to give me access on and off the patio area and subsequently on to the main pavement. The flat faced south west, so it got the sun from about midday and the little patio was quite private. It wasn't too far from the town or seafront, about ten to fifteen minutes. I put an offer in on the day, as suitable properties are so hard to find.

Carers would come in four times a day, getting up and breakfast, lunch, tea and bed, then if there was an emergency, I always had the thing around my neck. The builder/owner knew I was in a wheelchair

141

so he came back with a counteroffer, that he would raise the little patio area and put a ramp in, to enable me to get on and off the little patio area if I paid the asking price. I thought about it in a few moments and readily agreed. My mum was handling all voice contact, so I texted her.

My key worker was on holiday, so I relished the idea of welcoming her back with a poem, which I did:

So you had a little break
No more Tim for a week or so
No more jobs, or cheques to write
Just leave that to Kelly
Why worry, it's now her plight

Time off for moving house
It is a stressful thing
You need all the help you can get, that's true
Oh, by the way
What did Lisa and her sister do?

Do you have new neighbours?
Do they know what you and your family are like?
Don't sit still, good God
For if they have nice gardens
They might give you a floppy hat and rod

Your partner is back
I hope you were on your best behaviour
First impressions count, for goodness sake
No more feeble excuses like
Not tonight my dear, I have a headache

You will be pleased to know
No more cheques are needed
I have an account on eBay now
Just like your mum

I too, am a lazy male cow

You were sorely missed
I think not
Kelly did a good job, erm cough
So next time don't feel guilty
Like it says on my door, just BOG OFF!

Just so you thoroughly understand my sense of humour: my key worker is quite small, she moved house, I send funny e-mails to her mum, who has just got some home help and I have a notice on my door that says "Oh no not you...... now bog off!" (from the auction site again).

I had a meeting over at the flat, primarily to see if the space was workable. There was my mum and her partner, who had driven me over there, the estate agent, the builder-cum-owner, his assistant, who turned out to be his son, the OT that specialised in conversions, a council official, oh and me. The bathroom was the stumbling block, as it was so small. They all discussed how moving a wall or two (which was only stud) would give them more room to play with, in the bathroom that is. I must admit it was all over my head, but I did chime in with some useful suggestions. I never realised it was so involved and I hadn't secured it yet. After two hours a decision was made that just one wall need be altered by one foot, to give me the required space in the bathroom, without *really* affecting the rest of the flat. The OT and the council official needed to put their heads together, along with another specialist, who seemed to be situated at the council offices, so we all went on our merry way.

I updated my notice about me, as it had been some months since I did it. I tried to inject some humour into it, so it wouldn't be easily forgotten:

All carers

Please read

It's that silly time of the year again, Formula 1 is on, which means I will miss my meals if it is on.

Sometimes I cough, I very seldom choke now. The drinks make me cough, not choke, cough. Coughing is a natural reaction of my body, just trying to keep my airways clear, so it is a good thing. I cough because the consistency of blackcurrant is much thinner than juice. Why then have blackcurrant, I hear you say. Because I am a vain bastard, that's why. There, I have admitted it okay, are you happy now? I am more concerned with the calorific content than anything else. The best thing is to put one drink on my table, immediately in front of me and wait for me to ask for the other one. You can put the other one on a table that I am not using. How do you know if I am coughing or choking, I will tell you how. It is quite simple really. When I am drinking, I cough, when I am eating I choke. That is a rough guideline. If you're unsure, ask me, I will do a thumbs up when it's a cough, thumbs down means I am choking. Just leave me if I am coughing.

I can't tell the difference between wind and actually having a dump. If you're sitting down, you have the luxury of leaning to one side to fart. I, unfortunately, don't have that luxury.

I have a publisher for my book. It will be on Amazon as well as available in bookshops. I expect you to buy a copy! I will finish in about 6-8 weeks, I am up to nearly 48,500 words now. The publisher will take about 4 weeks. Just in case some of you can't work that out, don't expect to see anything before the end of June—beginning of July.

Test

(But please don't write your answers down, it is a verbal test not a written one)

What do I do when F1 is on?

_____

What can't I tell the difference between? _____ *and*
_____.

What will I do, if asked, when I am coughing?

_____

What will I do, if asked, when I am choking?

_____

Did you say it out loud? If you didn't, go back and do it again. If you did, who's the bloody idiot now, for talking to yourself? Be careful Ali doesn't admit you as a resident!

Can you put your initials in __a__ box, or put your mark if you can't write. That way Ali knows who's read it, although "marks" are bit harder for Ali to decipher.

(Ali is the Manager)

CHAPTER TWENTY-FOUR

Claudia was coming and I was waiting in the small hallway. I was already in my old chair for the week while she was there, as it fitted in the car better. It was late and I wondered if Giona would still be awake or would Claudia have to carry him in, as she had had to before. They were coming straight here after about six hours of travelling.

I had been there about half an hour, when I saw the security light come on and then I saw little Giona running up to the door, followed soon after by Claudia. I wasn't emotional, just overcome with joy. They would be here for Easter and Jacob's tenth birthday, which just so happened to be on Easter Sunday this year. May I just say that this little paragraph took me ages to write, because I was so emotional as I wrote it.

I practically shelved writing whilst they were here, although I did embellish some chapters.

I was Dad again, or Papa Tim to Giona. All little children are cute, but he was/is so very cute. With his longer than normal blonde hair and he would chatter away in Italian. It is surprising how much English he understood and if he really dug deep, he could say a lot of English too. He does anything to make you laugh, he loves being funny.

The next day, the afternoon to be precise, we made arrangements to go and see the flat. I think Claudia liked it. They have such big flats in Italy, no doubt she thought this one was quite small in comparison to hers.

We walked Derry the next day, all four of us that is. It was a dreary day, but most of the rain held off for us, Derry always waiting for Claudia.

After a good night's sleep, we all drove down to Plymouth, mainly to see my old speech therapist, if you remember they had moved, so it didn't really hold any memories for me.

We had lunch there and did lots of reminiscing before it was time to go.

On Thursday morning we had a progress meeting, whilst Giona played. Jacob had gone back to his mum's. The flat was discussed and nothing really could be done, until it was mine, but the OT had decided that the bathroom was workable, without having to disturb a wall. Which meant that there was much less work to do *should* I be successful in securing it, but it would still take about six months or more. No doubt it was all the red tape involved. Just in case you were wondering, the front door would be automatic, with a touch pad on the inside and a key pad on the outside. The windows were likely to be automatic as well. Marvellous what you can achieve with technology now.

That afternoon, we did the last of the birthday and Easter Sunday shopping. I must tell you what happened in the evening. We ate out, which is nothing strange, but whilst Giona was eating, some of the peas that were on his plate, fell on to the table, about six I think, then when the waitress took away his plate, along with everyone else's, all that was left were these six peas, which he started playing with intensely. One pea met with an accident (it was squashed), so he was left with five, which he continued to play with, along with chattering away, as children do, in his native language. To me it looked so funny, as he nudged these cold peas around the table, but I guess it loses a bit in translation, you really needed to be there and see him.

We went to Totnes one day, which if you know it, is quite narrow and on a hill. Everybody got out of my way, not that they had a choice, mind. On the way back to the car park, I decided to see if I could fit in an alleyway that had offset rails to deter cyclists. It saved all of thirty seconds, but I did it. It was practically by the car and Claudia and Jacob took turns in saying to Giona "Is your dad mad, stubborn, crazy, stupid?" and many more. They spoke in English and each time Giona would look at me, for me to nod "Yes" or shake my head "No" before giving his answer.

Meantime, we had reached the car and Claudia had opened it up for me to enter. I had found the conversation funny and when I tried to enter the car, up the slope, my amusement meant I couldn't hit the slope square on. This amused me even more. The more I tried, the more cock-ups I made, the more I uncontrollably laughed, much to everyone's amusement. Claudia had to take the control, I was in no fit state to do it.

The next day, Sunday, was a very eventful day: Easter Sunday and Jacob's tenth birthday. He got up early to go to the toilet, everyone was awake. Claudia was so thoughtful, she quickly got all his presents from the wardrobe, where I had been hiding them and put them under the bedcovers. When he emerged, Claudia told him it was too early and to get back in bed. He reluctantly agreed and went to pull the covers back, only to find his presents and cards. He spent about the next hour opening them. Next it was time for Easter, small chocolate eggs for the boys and some nice stone eggs for Claudia. That wasn't it, for I had got the boys a present each and a digital palm camcorder for Claudia, which will benefit us all really, but predominately for Claudia so she could film Giona and e-mail it to me. After breakfast and the boys perching themselves on the bed to watch an old film about a boy and an extraterrestrial that he befriends, we all went to my sister's. I was in a different chair this time (as it fitted in the car better), which was lighter and they had hired different ramps, these were solid, so it shouldn't be so dangerous as last time and it wasn't, it was much easier to get in and out. So much so that, after stuffing our faces, we all went outside for an Easter egg hunt and to watch the children play with flying balloons. Claudia fed a cow and was shocked to see how long its tongue was, then we went back inside to stuff our faces again. I ate so much, my tummy was aching, I didn't have any Irish cream this time, neither did I win at pass the parcel, I did last time.

Early the next morning Claudia and Giona were due to leave. Heaven knows when I will see them both again. I would miss them so much, we had had such a good time. It became all to much for me and I burst into a fit of sobbing just before they left in their taxi. I cried much of that morning, missing breakfast and I tried to sit quietly in my room, until lunchtime. I was at my table with my drinks in front of me, Claudia sent me a very personal text, which I read and it started me off crying again. I was in no fit state to have lunch or my drinks. I managed to get away from the table that was set up for me in the lounge, where I ate on my own, just lunchtime, Monday, Wednesday and Fridays (this was to see if I was okay at eating unsupervised). I scuttled back to my room, tears in my eyes. I was so emotional, I crashed the chair, ripping my arm pad very badly. I wouldn't have minded, but I was back in my other chair now. Because I crashed and damaged my chair, this made me more emotional. I managed to get back to my room and after sitting quietly for a little while, I pressed my bell to call the carers to put me on the bed, as I thought a rest would do me good. After all, I did look quite knackered , so I was told. I ate tea and had a little extra to drink, I was back on my diet again.

I read this through a few times and embellished a fair few of the chapters. I love that word, embellish. I will try not to use it too much from hereon in, but I do like it: embellish, embellish, embellish, embellish, embellish. Told you I liked it.

My key worker was doing one of her National Vocational Qualifications (N.V.Qs.) and part of her assessment was to get a statement from me, on what I thought of her, so I was only too eager to oblige. In my own style, of course:

Jackie,

Firstly I would have put her surname, but I don't bloody know it, it's bound to be something short anyway.

What is Jackie like as a carer? Now that would be telling, wouldn't it? Still, the shit has to hit the fan sometime, so it might as well be now.

Apart from leaving my leg bag open twice, which gave me a soggy foot, she is okay.

I keep her very busy, if she is not busy wrapping stuff for me, she is tidying my admin drawer, opening my post, cutting my nails (reluctantly), keeping my water feature topped up, doing some speech therapy work (time allowing), generally looking out for me and much more I could mention. So you see, she hasn't inherited her mum's lazy cow genes.

She doesn't know it, but she has given me some general ideas about life.

She likes to take the piss out of me when she can, which I don't mind. I give her plenty of stick anyway, like needing some miracle grow or smoking stunts your growth, oops too late.

Jackie is good at her job, she would have to be, to put up with my warped sense of humour.

On most things (except leg bags) she is ahead of the game, thoroughly understanding my needs.

Jackie does an awful lot for me and I don't know what I would do without her, after all, who else could I take the piss out of?

Tim Mason

P.S. Sorry about the colour, but I was running out of black ink.

(I wrote it in bright pink)

You can't hit it off with everybody, I suppose. You are bound to get a clash of personalities. There was one carer whose general attitude was very condescending, she always asked me, to say "Please" and "Thank you" which I would have said if I could, but when prompted, I just couldn't get my mouth to form a "P" or "T". Not that

I didn't appreciate what they did, far from it. "Thank you" was easier to say, but "Please" was so, so hard, it must be one of the hardest words to say. But to be prompted in a "childlike way" was too much, even if I found saying it hard. Whenever she had to do anything for me, she would "huff" and "tut" under her breath, like she didn't really enjoy her job (which she was good at).

Another senior care worker seemed to relish having an argument with me (probably because I was very stubborn and bolshie). She had a very nonchalant attitude, like she knew everything. She was always right (so she thought) and had an answer for everything, but even the Prime Minister gets it wrong sometimes (she should have gone into politics). Most days she was okay, it was just the odd day when she got out of the proverbial bed on the wrong side.

Generally though, they were all okay. I guess the care industry is one of the most demanding and most stressful jobs to be in. I think I could fill a chapter up with their faults, but I am sure that we, the residents, were just as bad.

I am still taking the cannabis, although I have to take so much now. I did very occasionally take it before my strokes and I needed so little to get high, I am surprised at how much I have to take to get the same effect. Before, I needed about two rice grains worth, now I need about half a thimble full. Needless to say, I don't get stoned very often. I must have got carried away with it one night: I watched a whole DVD completely stoned out of my head. I was so stoned that I thought I was actually in the film. I remembered it, although it did seem odd.

Oh, I forgot, Claudia bought me some individual foil-wrapped eggs from Italy. They were from her parents, and she and Giona unwrapped each individual one for me.

I was below some flats and the three individual occupants had moved on. Well, that's not exactly true: one had moved out to his own flat, one had to be in another room so he was more accessible and one, unfortunately, had died. The owner of the home had decided to

151

completely gut these flats and turn them into two en-suite rooms, two bedrooms and one bathroom. For weeks I had to put up with the workmen banging, sawing, drilling and generally crashing around. If it became too noisy, I would put my music on and turn it up a bit more than I would usually have it. They did some plumbing, or rather attempted to do some plumbing, for I had a very big drip, to say the least, coming down one of my light fittings (I had two) and making a "splat" on the carpet by my bed.

The workmen had gone home, but luckily the maintenance man was on hand to sort it out. Unfortunately, he made it much worse. A plumber was called out. Later that evening, because the water leak was under the floor boards and more had escaped than originally thought, it seeped into a smoke detector, setting it off. The bells went on for ages and in the distance I could hear the wail of the fire engines, making their way here. Meanwhile, the bells kept ringing. They were eventually stopped, by the firemen, once they had looked around the building and they were happy there was no fire. They located the smoke alarm and discovered it was full of water. I know all this, because they had a conversation about it, outside my door. The last time they came, it was also due to a faulty smoke detector, which just so happened to be mine. Claudia was here and Giona was so excited to have firemen *actually* in his room, I think that made his time here. Jacob (who happened to be staying that night) offered the burly firemen a chocolate. They replaced my faulty smoke detector, although I have no idea where it came from.

CHAPTER TWENTY-FIVE

I am right up to date now. I haven't heard any more about the flat, I think the council are waiting for me to complete a form and send it back, for the extra money, before they can take my application further. I tried to get someone to fill it in for me, but they were always too busy, or something cropped up. I hope I don't lose the flat. I eventually cajoled someone into doing it and sent it back.

Even now, some two years on, I still have occasional days when I get depressed. I just wish I could turn the clock back, but I can't, can I? This is totally irreversible, I will just have to adjust to my new life and put up with it. I may appear to be funny, but that's my way of dealing with my condition. Deep down I am sad for the life I lost and the fact I can't be a real, full-time dad and can't sleep next to Claudia and share her life.

I think one of the things I wanted on the long, long road to independence was total control of my bowels. It is totally embarrassing/humiliating for your body to catch you out. It didn't happen often, as I had my routine all planned out, but just occasionally I was caught out. This was going to be quite a big hurdle for me. How I overcome it, I just don't know, but I will.

I was asked if I would write some alternative lyrics to a song, as the lady who controlled the finances was leaving. Not that she didn't like the job, she had been there for six years and just felt it was time to move on. I had written some alternative lyrics before, for the staff to sing to the owner – this was at Christmas and it went down very well. I suppose the song I did was a little obscure, so I won't bore you with it. This time it was much more well known, being originally sung by a certain Swedish pop group, in the seventies I think. It took me all of two hours to do it. Not that I am boasting, I just find it relatively easy:

The Best That I Can Be

Oooh ooooh
You can count
You can type
Doing this wonderful job
Oooh
Answer the door
Look really keen
You are the Oldway queen

Friday night and it's time to go
Slogging all week don't you know
Doing things for Barry
Dealing with the cash
You've had enough of that

The only thing that keeps you sane
Is staring at Vin yet again
Fancying him so much
But your making promises
That your body can't keep
You wake up from your sleep
And you are the Oldway queen
Young and sweet only seventeen
Oldway queen
Now over the hill, but you can always dream

Oh yeah
You can count
You can type
Doing this wonderful job
Oooh
Answer the door
Look really keen
You are the Oldway queen

Dealing with residents all day long
Trivial things so you wish you were gone
So you have a new job

154

And you don't care

It's on Ali's agenda
But will you always remember
You were the Oldway queen
Young and sweet, only seventeen
Oldway queen
Now over the hill, but you can always dream

Oh yeah
You can count
You can type
Doing this wonderful job
Oooh
Answer the door
Look really keen
You are the Oldway queen

Lyrics by Tim Mason
You were the Oldway queen
Sung by everybody

I guess she was about mid-forties and idolised a certain "big built" film star, having his calendar in her office, a screen saver of him and loving any film he was in.

Because it was getting warmer (and therefore sunnier), I took myself into town, to pick a new pair of glasses. Not that there was much wrong with mine, but I did have some clip-on sun shades that made me look a right twat, if I went inside, say a shop, making me flip them up. These new ones darkened in sunlight and they were varifocals as opposed to my bifocals.

I had visited the optician's web site the night before and singled out a dark blue frame that I liked. I browsed the glasses and it wasn't too long before I was approached by one of their staff. She was very patient with me (as are all shop assistants), while I typed out the style

155

I had seen on their web site. She soon found the frames for me and she took me over to a booth, where she measured me up. They had a record of my prescription, as I had been there before for an eye test. Why I had an eye test there slips my mind at the moment, but I did. After I paid, I was asked if I could come back in two weeks, as they would be ready then. I was able to say "Thank you". Whether she understood me or not, I don't know. I made my way back to Oldway.

I went to the stroke group (S.C.O.P.E.—haven't the foggiest, what it stood for; thinking about it, it might have even been Scope) every Wednesday afternoon. It was a nice sunny afternoon and, as summer was now approaching rapidly, it was much warmer too. Anyway, I decided to make my own way back. It took me one hour, but it was nice. I had to come back via the seafront, as that was the most direct route. Not that I saw much of the sea, as I was too busy concentrating on my driving, avoiding people, slowing down when it was busy and generally being cautious. I was confident enough to stay in gear four, which I guess takes it up to about six miles per hour. I would normally have it on gear three, which is about walking pace, gear five being its top speed, eight miles per hour, which could just pass the average jogger. I would have loved to have taken my fleece off, but that was just not possible. I arrived back at the home, the same time as the transport from the stroke group arrived, as they had to drop off one other, as well as others on the way. I know the Manager was worried about my adventures, as she had visions of me having a crash and laying flat out on the pavement, so a compliment slip was taped to my board, that went with me everywhere, with my mobile phone and communication aid on it. I made my own way back many times, providing the weather was good. It still took me about one hour to get back, even though I upped the gear from four to five. I discovered what a difference raised pavements had; some pavements were so bumpy, not that you would notice if you were walking, but in a wheelchair I would really shake. You might notice the irregularity of some paths if you pushed a buggy or pram, so spare a thought for the little person that you are pushing. I feel every bump, so I am sure they can too. Tree roots were a problem, along with where workmen had been. Some were so bumpy I would have to stop and recover. When I went out shopping, some shops were a no-no, as they had steps that I couldn't negotiate. If this was the case and I needed something from a shop with a step, I would try my hardest to attract the shop assistants' attention, which is very difficult when you can't knock or wave.

If I didn't write (which wasn't often), I would play a game on my laptop which was so very absorbing that sometimes I would play one game for days. It was a race to build your own kingdom, destroy others, or be the first to "Alpha Centauri". As I said, it was very absorbing. There are not many games I know of that you can play with one hand.

I must tell you about one incident, about the carer that got her murds woddled, I mean her words muddled. One morning she asked me if I wanted a condom, instead of do I want a conveen. No, not that one, this one. When I went to bed at night, me being me, I had moisturiser put on my face, before I was transferred to my bed, where in the sitting position I could hold on to the sides of the bed, so the carers could take my clothes off and then swing me on to the bed, one being on my feet, the other on my shoulders. Cot sides they were called , that's what I held on to, they could be pulled up if necessary so you were safe in bed. Mine were just there so I could hold on and eventually I could hold on with both hands most nights, if you curled my right hand round the bar and helped me grip.

Now going back to the moisturiser, my key worker pointed out to me that my cuticles were dry and part of my beauty routine should be to have some moisturiser rubbed into the back of my hands, paying particular attention to my cuticles. This night, the carer put moisturiser on both sides of my hands. Thank goodness the Standaid had a belt that went round me, or I would have easily slipped off. There was no way I could hold on to the cot sides, although I did try once with my left hand, It just slipped right off.

I kept chasing for information about the flat, as I had done my bit. I was getting worried, in case the vendor got fed up with all the hassle. Eventually, by email from my solicitor friend, I was told to expect exchange of contracts in about six weeks, which the vendor was happy with. I think that when that happens it is a good time to finish this book. Although you may be happy for me, personally, I will feel happy when I have actually exchanged contracts. My solicitor friend was actually a conveyancer and with his legal experience had helped me out on umpteen things. He didn't really do conveyancing any more. I don't rightly know what he did, I only know that his new job took him away from his family through the week.

I regularly texted and emailed Claudia and sent attachments for Giona. I missed them so much. I phoned on occasion and was treated to Giona babbling down the phone to me in his native tongue. Claudia came on the phone to me and would tell me what he had just said. I wasn't due to see them until the summer, three months again. I accepted it was difficult for Claudia to keep taking time off work, it was just something I was going to have to get used to. She was coming with her parents this time, who I hadn't seen since February 2004, over two years earlier. Boy, was I going to be emotional. Normally Claudia came for just over a week. She had told me it would be shorter this time. She didn't tell me how short, but I anticipate about four or five days this time.

I got very, very frustrated with her on the phone, on occasions. I know it was difficult for her. If she found it difficult to understand a word, she would get me to spell it out, letter by letter, then she would repeat the letter back to me. Sometimes she didn't write the letters down, so she would get the word wrong and I would get frustrated and have to start again. Other times, she would just go silent at the end of the phone, because she didn't understand, as I repeated and repeated the letter, she was still quiet. This happened more when she was tired. This got me very frustrated and I would scream. I was trying so hard.

I started drinking just water at lunch and teatimes. I still kept to my juices at breakfast time. I would cough quite a lot with water, so I reluctantly agreed to have one teaspoon of thickener in it. It didn't make a lot of difference, but just enough to help my coughing a lot, although I did still cough on occasions. I didn't really want thickener, as I thought it was a step back. It didn't taste at all and was made of maize starch and the analysis on the tin proved its contents to be practically negligible.

I ate on my own every lunchtime now, apart from weekends. A bell extension was set up for me, so I could easily ring for help if necessary.

Oh, I nearly forgot: I started going weekly floating again. I was assessed quickly the week before and on the way back we dropped into another care home for me to be weighed (my idea). It was a similar one to the one they had at Rowans, only I had to be taken out of gear and pushed on, they got the total weight, then hoisted me out of the chair on to a nearby plinth and weighed the chair, then did their sums, I was just under eleven stone, before my strokes I was eleven and a half, I still considered myself to be fat, so I will still watch what I eat.

The pool was much older, but they had a hoist and water is water anyway. I was hoisted, on the pool side, out of my chair, on to the most uncomfortable, slatted, wooden table where two carers from the home got me ready for the water. Then the curtain that was pulled around me was opened, I was wheeled on the uncomfortable table, over to the hoist, the sling put around me again, then I was hoisted straight into the water for about thirty minutes of floating.

I only needed one carer with me in the water and one float around me.

I was offered a head support, but I didn't mind if my head trailed in the water, or the occasional bit of water went in my mouth, so I declined that. Can you move more in the water? I suppose you can, but any extra movement I achieved was negligible. I could just raise my legs though and the weight of them would make them sink for me, to agonisingly, lift them, slowly up again, I did this about twenty times, not that I was tired, as I never seemed to tire at anything, but because I thought that was long enough for the carer to stand still. They would drag me around the pool and they would make me sway or weave in the water. When the session was finished, I was hoisted out again, changed and straight home. There was no mandatory hot chocolate, chocolate bar or basket of chips.

CHAPTER TWENTY-SIX

T hank goodness the summer was practically upon us with the fairer weather. I had windproof coat and gloves, oh and trousers, but it was better going out in the warm and when the weather was fine. There was no way I could come back from stroke group on my own, if the weather was going to be inclement. True, I had a rain cover, but I felt such a numpty when that was put on me, I only wore it if I really had to. Like for a doctor's appointment, which was just down the road.

I can't begin to tell you how much I loved music. As I said before, the louder the better. Clubby, Italian, opera, old disco, ambient, some heavy rock, film scores, classical, ballads – it all inspired me. I had my favourites and would turn the volume up for them. I had such a good sound system, some tracks would make me shiver. I mostly got my music ideas from my memory or if I heard something on the radio that was played each morning in the dining room and it took my fancy, I would make a mental note and then download it later.

I was still having problems with my e-mail and I sent many e-mails to my internet provider, even via my brother, so there is no excuse, but still they didn't bother to contact me.

I think I will change suppliers when I can, as I believe they are now in breach of contract. A friend was looking into changing it for me.

I put together a box full of goodies for Claudia and Giona that were packed and later posted by my key worker: temporary tattoos, stickers, model cars, bubble liquid, flying balloons, chocolate covered finger wafers, kids' liquid paracetamol, adult headache tablets, kids' clothes, a blackcurrant drink, a DVD, two chocolates and a car sponge with a smiley face.

The Best That I Can Be

I am bang up to date now, writing about things that happened, or things I did, just a couple of days ago. I still keep adding bits in here and there.

Squeaky's fingernails were getting long now. I am sure he must have access to some nail clippers or scissors. If it isn't his thumbnails, it is his fingernails. If they are now a couple, why doesn't Gummy nag him about it? Some partner she is!

I went into town and got my new glasses. I had a fitting, to make sure they fitted okay, then I went out in the sun and they darkened, which was cool. I then hunted round the town for a particular shop that I could easily gain access to. I found one but it had two steps, there was no way I could negotiate those steps. "There must be another one," I thought to myself. I went everywhere in the town, until I found one, up by the seafront, that I could easily access. I must point out that I had one before my strokes. I went in and asked if I needed an appointment. I didn't, and the chair that is normally used was moved so I could access the sterile area. They explained how much it was and that they only did one type, which I was shown. I approved. The man who was doing it asked me if I was ready. I think they used a clamp, then they drove the special needle in, which only hurt for a split second, the ornate piece hurt more when it was put in. He then showed me my new eyebrow piercing in a mirror. It was silver and in my left eyebrow. It would need bathing with salt water, but that could easily be included in my beauty regime. You couldn't feel it once it was in and I had a bit of a black eye for a few days though. They were so nice in the shop, two operatives and one middle-aged man, who was having a tattoo done, to go with his many others. They were all very curious about my condition and gave me time to type out the answers to their questions.

I shocked everyone back at the home. Most of them said I was brave and they were squeamish.

These new varifocals were so much better, apart from if I was reading for a long time, when I used my very cheap reading glasses. The varifocals had such a narrow area for reading, it was a strain to

162

hold my head up to see the laptop screen. They were okay for reading things on my lap, like my communication aid or phone, but it was just too much to hold my head up while I typed. Then I hit on the idea of my cheap reading glasses that were bought buy my mum.

I don't think I have told you about the nail on my other big toe. I noticed it was dead at Christmas time. It didn't hurt and was firmly attached to the nail bed and was slowly being pushed off by my new nail. it was cut quite regularly by the visiting chiropodist who incidentally was Irish and had been given a typical Irish name as a nickname, poor girl.

I hated doing my weights, probably because they were ladies' weights and their weight was a mere fraction of what I used to lift and that was a struggle. Still, I did it. Every other day, apart from weekends, two repetitions, until I decide that I would do one repetition every day and just see how I get on.

I started doing some kind of sit-ups. They were not as you know sit-ups, as I was already sitting up in my chair. I would grimace as I made an attempt to pull myself forward, I could if I was already sitting up. Then after about thirty, I would fully incline the chair. There was no way I could sit up from that position, but I would go through the motions anyway, just attempting to tense my stomach muscles, then, after about twenty, I would sit back up and try some more in that position. As I was concerned about my appearance (I was putting on weight around my middle), I thought these would help.

My sneezes were so ferocious, which was a big problem if I was at my table. "ACHOO" the table would be shunted, the plate would move, disturbing the food and my drink, if there was one on my table – as I got the carers to only put one on my table, until I was ready for the next one, which was placed on the main table. My drink would slop everywhere. I soon learnt that if I pinched my nostrils, I could prevent myself from sneezing – if I was quick enough and got to my nostrils in time, that is. They sort of got hot, that's how I knew I was going to sneeze.

I had speech therapy once every week. Sometimes we would just talk about what's been happening, other times I had to practice single words or short phrases. She thought I had dramatically improved over the months and I was too hard on myself, but, as I said, I am sure that not being happy with my improvement gave me the impetus to keep improving.

As it looked like me moving into my own flat was a certainty, I decided to take stock of my monthly expenditure. I discovered, much to my horror, that I was spending far more than the benefits I was getting (I was only entitled to two whilst I was in a care home, but I was entitled to much more if I lived out). I stopped my weekly massage and my twice monthly acupuncture. I also stopped my monies to Jacob and Giona, collectively, that would save me nearly three hundred pounds a month. I fully intended to start them again, IF I could when I knew about and was receiving my benefits, when I moved into my own place. That's the trouble with this country, they would take fairly good care of you as an individual, but didn't give a damn about your dependants, including your partner, whether you were married or not. It is only you they are interested in, as I said. You can't even palm off some of your money, as that is classed as disposing of assets. Frustrating, isn't it?

My DVDs that were posted to me took one week before they sent them back to me and they say that three others I sent back were lost in the post. Regardless of their excuse, I had had enough. Half of them kept jumping anyway, even though I got the carers to thoroughly clean them. I sent them the rudest email you can imagine. They promised they would stop collecting money from my account forthwith and credit back any monies due. I wouldn't get any more, I would just rely on my two comical friends to get some.

I got a phone call from Claudia – well, it was Giona actually, thanking me for the box of goodies. I could just hear Claudia in the background, prompting him in English, while he repeated word for word down the phone to me. Apparently he screamed with delight when he saw it.

The masseuse was always trying to get me to drink water and eventually, with a teaspoonful of thickener, I did (I coughed violently without it). Although I was adamant with the speech therapist that I wouldn't use thickener again, as I saw it as a step back, but I could see her and the Manager's concerns, so I did. I told the masseuse it was thickened and she, being the "alternative, nagging" mother hen that she is, suggested something natural. Psyllium husks, a by-product of linseed oil, thickened drinks disgustingly and also helped your bowels. Neither of the thickeners tasted, nor left any aftertaste, it's just that the psyllium husks, which I took at teatime every other day, resembled watery frogspawn. It even had little black bits in it, which didn't help the mind one little bit, but so long as you didn't look at it, it was okay. Maybe, just maybe, it will help me to control my bowels. I have only just started taking it, so I will let you know.

The colour went on my DVD player, which seems ironic when I had just cancelled my DVD membership. It wasn't really warranted, as I bought it from the auction web site. Serves me right for buying a cheap one. I did buy another one, still cheap and again from the auction web site. It was still a famous name, but this time it was new and came with a manufacturer's warranty of twelve months.

I was getting fed up with the bike, I just didn't seem to be making any headway. What could I do? Then I hit on the idea of going against it. Don't forget, it was automated. I could programme it to automatically change direction. One minute I was pedalling, conventionally forwards, five minutes later it would change direction so I was pedalling backwards and I would try my hardest to stop it, get the idea... Boy, did I feel my thigh muscles burn. There was no way of monitoring if I was improving, as the bike would only register if I was going with it, which I wasn't. Maybe, it will help me burn off some of that excess fat around my middle, or have I got to accept it as part of my condition? The carers didn't think I was fat, but I did, maybe that's why I watched what I ate – very carefully, I might add. I don't think it's bad for men to take care of themselves, but maybe I was a little excessive. I still don't think that's a bad thing.

One morning I went swimming and it was a very eventful morning. In the early hours the swimming pool had suffered a power cut and the staff had to put the pool heater back on, so the water wasn't up to temperature (it felt so cold to me, particularly because I was practically motionless), then when we got back to the home, I was reversing down the slope from the car and I completely forgot that I was in the old chair, which has a tendency to tip back and therefore I should always have someone behind me. There wasn't and I tipped right back, crashing to the floor. I was laughing so much at my predicament. The two carers that were with me weren't, they both had coronaries. I was righted back up the right way, with me laughing. There was no damage done and I was okay. My mobile phone was okay, as was my communication aid, which had hit me on the chin as I fell. An accident report form was filled out though. Someone will be behind me in future.

We were in my car, as there was four of us. My car had four seats, while theirs only had two. They did have a minibus as well, but that wasn't available to us, so instead of them ordering a taxi each week for the fourth person, I offered the use of my car. Actually, they were doing me a favour, as it meant my car was being used once a week, instead of lying idle in between Claudia coming over.

I was a bit surprised, to say the least, when one of my comical friends (who happened to be a mechanic and who owned his own business) took my old car, to give it a new MOT, then texted me sometime later to say he had sold it. It was only worth about £600. He never texted me back to say that the sale had fallen through. As he had been unwell, I hadn't seen him for some weeks, then when I did see him, I realised he hadn't sold it. It was a nice little car as well, a diesel turbo hatchback, in good condition, with relatively low mileage compared to its age. I eventually just gave it to my sister and her husband. They already had two cars, which they needed, but were getting rid of one of them, as it had proved to be unreliable and it refused to start. They were a bit strapped for cash and were very grateful. I didn't ask for any money for it, although they did offer some. I didn't want it.

CHAPTER TWENTY-SEVEN

Hey, guess what? Claudia had decided to stay on after her parents, who would stay in a local guesthouse. She would stay for an extra two weeks or so, after her parents had gone back. Can you imagine how happy that made me? I am sure it will really devastate me, when she and Giona go back. That is due to happen after I finish this book, so think of me. I know, I know, you will be reading this a long time after they went back, but still spare a thought for me though.

It is devastating when you catch a cold or a bug in my situation. Normally you would just muddle through a cold, but you are so vulnerable when you're like this, you just have to put up with whatever your body throws at you. Half the time, you don't know that you have even picked up a bug.

I have just started a variation on my sit-ups, so I don't cheat and use what strength I have in my legs to pull me forward (remember they are strapped on the footplates). I have my footplates taken off (so my legs dangle), then I do my sit-ups, along with leg raises. Well, they are not really leg raises, as I only bend from the knee, but I do practically extend both legs and then gravity pulls them back down again. Something else I have just started, when I am on the toilet: I am able to do side bends, as I am strapped to the Standaid, so I am prevented from leaning over too much (so I don't fall off). I do about twenty of these. It is difficult to do it in the chair, as the chair arms get in the way, as does the back support (I have tried, obviously).

It took bloody days to find a suitable (cheap) DVD player on the auction web site. I found two, only to be outbid at the last minute by another bidder. I eventually got one, not exactly what I wanted, but it was very cheap and came with a twelve month warranty, so I mustn't complain.

I am waiting for confirmation that I have exchanged. Anyway, I am right up to date, so regardless of what happens I am close to the end. Should I be successful, I am thinking of getting a cat. It will have to be an adult one, of course, with an easy name for me to try and say. I just hope it has good hearing.

I made myself a list of items I will need if I am going to be living independently in that flat:

Things I will need Immediately

Wardrobe	100
Drawers (might not need them if wardrobe and desk have drawers)	50
Drawers for TV in bedroom	50
TV combi	169
Desk of some sort, maybe a dressing table style	50
Curtains (Drop?)	10
Plates etc.	10
Cutlery	30
Kitchen utensils	10
Pans	40
Bibs	30
Eating table	50
Cups	2
Food	80
Iron and ironing board	15
Toaster	10
Kettle	10
Mugs for visitors	5
Total	721

Later

Zedbed for Claudia	30
Bunk beds	50
Chair for boys' room (beanbag)	20
1 quilt and cover, other one can be mine	5
Beanbag for lounge	<u>20</u>
Total	125

Cat	20
Flap	20
Feeder	20
Water thingy	10
Misc	<u>30</u>
Total	100

My mum would supply me with a vacuum cleaner, maybe I will be given other things from my list. I was lucky, as there was already a cooker, fridge and washer/drier in the flat, so I didn't have to worry about that. I am sure there are some things I have forgotten, but some things I already have here. I would get ALL the things I needed from the auction web site, as I had discovered you could get anything from there and they were quite cheap as well, even though you had to pay postage on top of the price, it was still cheap.

Actually, I have been thinking: maybe I don't need a cat flap, the cat can just use the automatic door I will have.

My key worker went caravanning for the bank holiday weekend, so I saw that as a golden opportunity to write something for when she got back:

The Best That I Can Be

Camping at the weekend
I hope you had lots of fun
With lots of grass and cow pats
Sticking up ya bum!

I'm not a hardened camper
You wouldn't catch me in a tent
I like my little luxuries
Even if I do pay more rent!

Why did I agree to come?
Who's idea was it anyway?
I think I made a rash decision
Oh, why didn't I stay!

This camping lark isn't bad
Apart from the washing up
There's always something missed you need
Like a plate, bowl or cup!

Oh, that outdoor air
Making you feel fresh
Is that a rain cloud I can see?
Oh, I hope we don't get wet!

The facilities are great
I can even dry my hair
Shall I bother with that task?
Or give the neighbours a scare!

It's romantic at night
Though it's dark and cold you see
I just wish he could be romantic
And put his arm round me!

I've had enough now
How I yearn for my own bed

Somewhere comfortable to lay down
And place my weary head!

I am not cut out for camping
So, if I am asked again next year
I will reply, "I don't feel well,
So, can we give it a miss, my dear?"

Yes, she liked it and as usual, took it home to show her family.

I am still just waiting for confirmation of the exchange. I know the searches have been done and the solicitors are happy with that. It's 99% mine, but I will only be completely happy when it is confirmed it is 100% mine.

I am glad I have nearly finished anyway, as I am fed up with feeling guilty when I go out to enjoy the summer. I can just enjoy it this year. I love the sun and readily soak it up any chance I can. As I said, it's very rare I burn. I go pink, but seldom burn.

The Manager, whom I had grown very fond of and I respected, was giving up the position of Manager and was going to be a full-time trainer/assessor. She was still going to be working here for the proprietor, in her new capacity, though on a very part-time basis. I know she wouldn't be based here anymore, only coming in occasionally. I was asked if I wanted to contribute to her "Moving over" present, but I, as always, did my own thing. I bought her a nice silver bangle, it was like a charm bangle really, with seaside charms dangling from it. It was quite unusual. She liked it and gave me a kiss. I was introduced to the new Manager, who seemed equally as nice.

Why is it you are promised something, then after waiting and waiting, nothing gets done? Time and again I was promised that something would be done in my room, only for the carer to then decide they were not going to do it (so I was told, much later), but no one told me. It's only because I waited and waited, then decided to chase up the carer, only to be told they were not going to do it. So why agree to do it in the first place and why not inform me of their decision?

Two years on now and I still ask myself "Why me?". I accept that I will always be disabled and I need help, but I refuse to accept my condition. I can always keep improving.

CHAPTER TWENTY-EIGHT

S orry, but this will be the last chapter. As part of the solicitor's regulations, as I had changed from my solicitor friend (he worked away and couldn't really devote enough time to my purchase), the new solicitors that he recommended needed some identification of who I was, before they could act for me, and one of the things they asked for was my passport, which I always kept in a drawer under the television. I asked my key worker to get it out. She couldn't, as it wasn't there.

My will and log book for my old car had gone missing from that drawer some months before, but I didn't think anything of it. But now with my passport missing, I did. My key worker searched all my drawers, the back, underneath them and my filing system. Nothing was found. Luckily, the solicitors accepted other identification than what was originally stipulated. The police were eventually called and they came immediately, but on hearing the story, they decided they would like to interview my key worker at the same time, so they made an appointment to come back when she was on shift, two days later. They didn't turn up. A call was made on my behalf and they apologised and made a further appointment, again two days later and again they didn't show up. This was a Friday and my key worker wasn't in until the Monday. Monday was no good, as I was due to go swimming and my key worker came with me and so a third appointment was made for Tuesday, just hope they show up this time. Tuesday is next week, so I can't yet tell you how it went. I can show you what I am going to give them **IF** they show;

Re—passport, will and duplicate log book

As I don't really speak, I wrote this, which should be helpful.

Firstly, let me say how disgusted I am that it has taken you three attempts to come down, not keeping the first two appointments. This incident was reported over a week ago. I could write all sorts of things, but I won't. Let's just say, I expected more and I am very disappointed.

Now you are here, read on.

All my documents are kept under the TV in the little drawer, on the right. Most carers, if not all, know they are there, or at least that's where I keep things, like letters (until they are filed), cheque book and things I may need.

Nothing has been taken by my family for safe keeping, they are aware of this situation. No solicitor has them either. I am not always in my room.

My solicitor friend, put the will and duplicate log book in the drawer, I saw him. It was a duplicate, as I had lost the original since my strokes, so I believed they were still there, although I noticed they were missing some months before the passport incident. I just thought they were missing and would eventually show up.

I applied yet again for another duplicate log book, as I was selling the car, which was soon put in my filing system, until I needed it.

On the 22nd of April, I needed a form of ID for the Abbey, as I was registered at Newton Abbot but needed to make a withdrawal from Paignton. I took my passport, that was the last time I saw it. It was definitely given back to me, but I have had Jackie phone the branch just in case. It is possible that it could have been dropped.

I first noticed it was missing about two weeks ago now, as I am buying a flat and the solicitor asked me to send some ID.

Since then Jackie has conducted a thorough search of all drawers, including the back and underneath and all filing boxes, but hasn't turned anything up.

Then, you were called.

I think the passport address is: 12, Highweek Road, Newton Abbot. Although my last residence was: 72a, Fore Street, Bovey Tracey.

Log book is in the Bovey Tracey address.

Will address is here.

Before I finish, I must tell you about one adventure I went on. Well, you know I have a super duper chair... It needed a good test of its durability and range. Currently I live on the coast in Preston, about a mile from Paignton town centre (that's Devon by the way). I made a decision to go to Brixham, just over six and a half miles away. Where there was a path, I went on it, unless it was on the other side of the road and traffic made it to difficult to get to, in which case, or if there was no path, I drove against the traffic. It took me two and a half hours. What about my leg bag I hear you say, as it only had a certain capacity? Don't worry, I had that covered.

As it happened, in Brixham I saw what looked like a care worker saying goodbye to her boyfriend. I approached her and asked her if she worked in a care home. I had just past it, she said. I asked her if she could empty my leg bag and call Oldway and tell them where I was and that I was okay, as I don't think they knew exactly where I was. Oh, and that I would be back about 8.30. I went down to Brixham harbour for about an hour, before heading off back. I must say the two and a half hours ahead of me seemed daunting, but it soon went. Driving in the road wasn't a problem for me either. I got back just in time for my ice cream at 8.45. Gosh, my left hand didn't half ache, from constantly pushing the control. I don't think I will do it again, I just wanted to prove a point to myself. They couldn't believe where I had been, when I got back, let alone that I had gone to another care home to get my leg bag emptied. Well, I ask you, what was I supposed to do? I am currently planning more trips, although not as far—yet!—and I am looking up residential homes in that area, to empty my leg bag.

Oh, the police did come. Nothing much was done, just a statement was taken. I must admit, I was worried they would open some drawers, so I buried my cannabis well. As it was a new batch, there was quite a lot and I was worried they would think I was a right druggy. As it happened, they didn't do any searching, thank goodness.

I am even closer to exchange now, as I just signed my contract and returned it to the solicitors, along with my deposit money. So I am anticipating exchange any day now.

I was very cold and felt very weak. I went to bed mid-morning, missing lunch. It is very, very unusual for me to feel the cold like that. I had two blankets. My blood pressure was taken and it was found to be low. The doctor was called and he found nothing wrong with me and recommended that I have a course of antibiotics. By bedtime, my blood pressure was back to normal.

Originally I was told to get some rest and sleep, but I gave up. First one carer came into give me some post, then another carer came in with the two blankets, then a carer came in and took my temperature, then she came back to take my blood pressure, then another carer came in with my lunchtime pills, then a cleaner came in to empty my bin, then the Manager came in to tell me the doctor had been called, then the doctor came in with the Manager. The doctor recommended some antibiotics as I said, to clear my system out, as he couldn't find anything wrong with me. Then a carer came in with my antibiotics and also recommended some food and drink, so she went out and came back with some food and a drink, so I gave up. I was still weak, but felt well enough to get up for tea, which by now it was (so much for my rest). My room was like bloody Piccadilly Circus.

I forgot that antibiotics play havoc with your body and they did.

I liked the new Manager and whenever she was in her office, which I could just see into, or if I saw her out and about, I would stick two fingers up at her and she would reciprocate and stick her middle one up at me.

I lost my eyebrow piercing. I haven't for the life of me got a clue where it went. I remember it being in my eyebrow at night, when I was put to bed. The next day, one carer noticed it was missing, when I came in from sun bathing in the garden. Oh well, I will just have to go through that excruciating pain again, when I eventually move I think. The exchange seemed to me to drag on and on and on and I was going to end the book there, but you will just have to buy the next book to see if I do exchange and complete. I think I am nearly there, but who knows what can happen in the maze of buying a property.

As I said in the beginning, I really hope you have enjoyed reading this as much as I have enjoyed writing it. I hope I have shown you that your independence and family are so important. Well, they are to me anyway. This could happen to you, so beware.

You can always email me at my hotmail address, disabled_tim@yahoo.co.uk. I will be more than happy to receive your questions or comments. I suppose thinking about it, I am amazed at myself for writing this much. As I said, I must have had the ability before and just didn't know it.

Still, they say out of something bad comes something good. Don't forget, if you are a tight arse and you have borrowed this book and you're interested in my welfare, go out and buy your bloody own, I get a percentage of that! You could always lend it to someone (ha ha). Go on, make a note now, before you forget.

I think I will write again, as I have thoroughly enjoyed this. I am sure it has helped me to come to terms with my condition. If nothing else, I have improved my spelling, and it keeps my mind active, which can't be a bad thing, in my situation. Apart from that, what else would I do with my time? This has been so absorbing. It has only taken me two years to write all this, which, so I am led to believe, is quite good by literary standards. Yes, I will write again. I have even thought of a title: "Life After Life" – at least that's what I plan to call it. Do you like it? So look out for it, won't you.

I have enjoyed remembering. I have come such a long way, from just eye movement to where I am now. I know I can achieve much more and I will endeavour to do it, for me, for Claudia and for my family. I don't think I am anything special. Far from it, I just have a lot to say, I miss conversation, I miss my family. God knows how much I miss Claudia and I miss life. I love Claudia so much. I am so, so sorry I am like this and her life is totally messed up now, all thanks to me, but I am so happy she is always beside me, even though she is still crap at kite flying. Her love makes me write, that's why I dedicate my book to her. I know if she was not in my life, there would be no book. My recovery has been because of her. She makes me so determined in my new life.

Where does the story end? My story goes on and on. It's this story that ends.

Do I see an end? I don't think so. Will Claudia always be beside me? I am sure she will. Will I ever get to Rome? I don't think so, but I sincerely hope so.

I just want my life back. It will never be the same, I know. I just want to be *the best that I can be.*

Printed in the United Kingdom
by Lightning Source UK Ltd.
114274UKS00001BA/135